P9-BZV-667

9646502

DMACC ECC
9076502

Dedication

I dedicate this book to early childhood professionals everywhere
who understand the value of child's play.

Acknowledgments

Once again, I offer my gratitude to the Gryphon House family. Special
thanks go to Larry and Leah, for heading the family with such heart and
humor; to Cathy Calliotte and Faustino Nuñez, for being delightful and
for their superb marketing abilities; and to my editors, Kathy Charner
and Kate Kuhn, for their warmth, wisdom, and encouragement! Thanks
always to Richard, Tootsie, and Freddy, for lighting up my life with love
and laughter.

Photographs were taken at the YMCA Silver Spring Child Development
Center in Silver Spring, Maryland. Special thanks to Lori Schantz,
Assistant Director, and teachers: Javiel Berrios, Helen Haile, Mary Harvey,
Evelyn Rutayuga, and Dee Dee Weaver.

Author Availability

Rae Pica is nationally recognized for her lively and enlightening
presentations. To arrange for staff development training, conference
workshops, or keynote speeches, contact her through Gryphon House,
or at raepica@movingandlearning.com.

Great Games

for Young Children

Over **100** Games to Develop Self-Confidence, Problem-Solving Skills, and Cooperation

Rae Pica

Illustrations : Kathy Ferrell
Photographs: Mary Duru

gryphon house, inc.
Beltsville, Maryland

© 2006 Rae Pica
Printed in the United States of America.

Published by Gryphon House, Inc.
10726 Tucker Street, Beltsville, MD 20705
301.595.9500; 301.595.0051 (fax); 800.638.0928 (toll-free)

Visit us on the web at www.ghbooks.com

All rights reserved. No part of this publication may be reproduced, stored in a retrieval system or transmitted in any form or by any means, electronic, mechanical, photocopying, recording or otherwise, without the prior written permission of the publisher.

Gryphon House is a member of the Green Press Initiative, a nonprofit program dedicated to supporting publishers in their efforts to reduce their use of fiber sourced forests. For further information visit www.greenpressinitiative.org

Library of Congress Cataloging-in-Publications Data

Pica, Rae, 1953-
  Great games for young children : over 100 games to develop self-confidence, problem-solving skills, and cooperation / Rae Pica; illustrations, Kathy Ferrell ; photographs, Mary Duru.
      p. cm.
  Includes bibliographical references and index.
  ISBN-13: 978-0-87659-006-5 (alk. paper)
  ISBN-10: 0-87659-006-7 (alk. paper)
 1. Games. 2. Self-esteem in children. 3. Problem solving in children.
I. Title.
  GV1203.P52 2006
  793.01'922--dc22

                              2005030568

Bulk purchase

Gryphon House books are available for special premiums and sales promotions as well as for fundraising use. Special editions or book excerpts also can be created to specification. For details, contact the Director of Marketing at Gryphon House.

Disclaimer

Gryphon House, Inc. and the author cannot be held responsible for damage, mishap, or injury incurred during the use of or because of activities in this book. Appropriate and reasonable caution and adult supervision of children involved in activities and corresponding to the age and capability of each child involved, is recommended at all times. Do not leave children unattended at any time. Observe safety and caution at all times. Every effort has been made to locate copyright and permission information.

Table of Contents

Chapter 3 Musical Games .61

Chapter 4 Cooperative Games 83

Introduction

Something Played for Fun

As I was setting up for a staff development workshop one night, I overheard one teacher tell another about a little girl who'd had a terrible crying jag over being eliminated from a game of Simon Says. The second teacher clucked in sympathy and the conversation moved on from there. There was no discussion of the fact that perhaps the game should be modified in the future so it didn't make children feel bad—that the intention of a game is to have fun.

You've witnessed it yourself, I'm sure: Children chosen last for teams; children sitting against the wall, watching forlornly as their classmates continue to play Hot Potato without them; and children who engage in the most atrocious behaviors to ensure they're not the ones eliminated from a game of Musical Chairs.

What constitutes a game? It's a word that's almost as difficult to define as the word *play,* which is what we do with games. According to Merriam-Webster Online, a game is an "activity engaged in for diversion or amusement." The Encarta Dictionary calls it "something played for fun."

Go to a website of game ideas for parents and you'll find descriptions of these activities and others like them. Parents make note of them and arrange for them to be played at birthday parties and play dates without a second thought as to the inappropriateness of eliminating and/or humiliating children. They themselves participated in these games when they were children, and they see no reason not to perpetuate the tradition.

As early childhood professionals, however, don't we have a responsibility to do more than perpetuate traditions? Because we've been entrusted with the education of the whole child, shouldn't we regard the activities we present in light of what they offer children in all domains of development—cognitively, socially, emotionally, and physically? Shouldn't we select games, just as we select the other parts of the curriculum, based on whether they are developmentally appropriate?

The Hall of Shame

Bredekamp and Copple (1997, p.10) note that development in one domain impacts development in the others. They explain, "Because developmental domains are interrelated, educators should be aware of and use these interrelationships to organize children's learning experiences in ways that help children develop optimally in all areas and that make meaningful connections across domains."

As teachers, we should choose games not only because they give children something to do, but also because they have something to teach. We may not initially think of games in terms of learning for children—perhaps, more often, as a break from learning—but children learn from all their experiences. It's up to us to decide what we'd like them to learn from the games we play with them: things like self-confidence, problem solving, cooperation, trust, and motor skills, or "rejection, competition, failure, and humiliation" (Staley and Portman, 2000, p. 67).

Dr. Neil Williams is the creator of The Physical Education Hall of Shame, a list of childhood games he considers inappropriate for physical education (PE) classes. Games that make this list share some of the following problems:

- Absence of the purported objectives of the activity or game.
- Potential to embarrass a child in front of the rest of the class.
- Focus on eliminating children from participation.
- Extremely low participation time.
- Extremely high likelihood for danger, injury, and harm. (Williams, 1994)

Williams (1994, p. 17) states: "As professionals, we must reexamine our practices and programs and think critically about what, how, and why we are teaching the children in our care." Currently, the Hall of Shame includes:

Dodgeball
Duck, Duck, Goose
Messy Backyard
Kickball
Musical Chairs
Relay Races

Steal the Bacon
Line Soccer
Red Rover
Simon Says
Spud
Tag

According to Bredekamp and Copple (1997, p. 14), "Play provides a context for children to practice newly acquired skills and also to function on the edge of their developing capacities to take on new social roles, attempt novel or challenging tasks, and solve complex problems that they would not (or could not) otherwise do." None of that is likely to happen while a child is battling (literally) to stay in the game or sitting miserably against a wall.

About This Book

Obviously, some games have more to offer children in one domain than in another. That's okay. But at the very least, we should remember the primary definition of a game and ensure that it's fun—for everyone. With all the stress in children's lives today, fun is perhaps the best reason to play games.

The games I've chosen or invented for this book provide benefits for the whole child. This means that if a game doesn't have something to offer in all three domains of child development, I didn't include it here. Some of my choices, like Statues, were already developmentally appropriate. Others needed a bit of tweaking to make them so. Still others, like Hot Potato and Musical Chairs (cited earlier), needed a serious overhaul before I could include them here.

Many of the games in this book involve group participation. Some require partners to work together. And some, like Hopscotch, involve one child taking a turn while others wait for theirs. In these cases, I've included suggestions to reduce waiting time. It's true that children must learn to wait their turn; it's a necessary social skill. However, waiting does not come naturally to young children and shouldn't be imposed on them too often. Besides, a child who is waiting is not physically participating and, therefore, not reaping all possible benefits!

I'm a big believer in all that play has to provide children, and I worry that, in this age of "academics" and "accountability," children are getting fewer and fewer opportunities to play. To help ensure play continues to be part of the early childhood curriculum, I've included a list of benefits in all three domains with each game. My hope is that the more rationale we have for children playing, the more we can fight against inappropriate practices—and the more we can help parents, administrators, and policy makers understand that play is what's best for the children!

Using This Book

I've organized the games in *Great Games* into five categories: Circle Games, Concept Games, Musical Games, Cooperative Games, and Outdoor Games. Naturally, there's some overlap among these categories. For instance, Musical Chairs is a musical game, a circle game, and (here) a cooperative game. But, to me, it's the use of music that most distinguishes it, so I've placed it in Musical Games. Similarly, games like Follow the Leader can certainly be played outside (and occasionally should be), but it's not first and foremost an outdoor game so I haven't placed it in that section.

Most of the games in this book can be played in 5- to 15-minute time frames (although you can certainly choose to play them for longer periods). As you know, much will depend on the children you're working with: how many there are, their ages and stages of development, how much experience they've had organizing themselves into groups, and so on.

Some games, such as Body Balance (in Cooperative Games), can be played in five minutes or less—when the children need a change of pace or you need to keep them briefly occupied. I've noted these with the words "Quick Pick." Those games that will likely require more than 15 minutes to play are marked with the words "Takes Time." Let's Make a Machine, also under Cooperative Games, is one example.

If you have a large indoor space available to you, you might also choose to note which of the games listed in Outdoor Games can be played indoors as well. Mother, May I? and Red Rover are two possibilities. Which will expend the most physical energy on a rainy or wintry day when the children are feeling cooped up? Games such as Follow the Leader and Choo-Choo, for instance, can be made as lively as you need them to be.

Which games might align well with a theme you're exploring? (For example, "Row, Row, Row Your Boat," in Musical Games, and Choo-Choo, in Concept Games, are both appropriate for a transportation theme.) Which are the best games for early in the year, when the children are getting to know one another? (This Is My Friend, in Circle Games, is perfect for learning one another's names. And the Cooperative Games generate friendly feelings among groups and between partners!)

If you have children with special needs in your class, you should make note of which games they can play without modification, and which will have to be adapted. For example, children with hearing impairments can play most of the games as written. However, when a game involves a signal or listening cues, hand signs may be necessary. Children in wheelchairs can often take part in games like Follow the Leader, Wall Ball, and Messy Backyard; but modifications may be needed in some of the tag games, for example.

Because "special needs" can include such a wide range of disabilities, it's difficult to address possible modifications for all games and all disabilities. I have, however, included a list of helpful resources at the end of the book ("Resources for Playing with Children with Special Needs"), in the hope that all children can be included in these game experiences.

Each game is organized in the same format. The game's benefits fall under "Why It's a Great Game" (why play the game) and are separated according to the three developmental domains: cognitive (cited, simply, as "for cognitive development"), affective ("for social/emotional development"), and physical ("for physical development").

The section titled "How to Play" provides instructions for playing. In the majority of games, you'll find there's no equipment needed—just the children's bodies and minds! When a game does call for equipment, you're generally only required to provide such common props as a parachute, balls, beanbags, or plastic hoops. Finally, if there are variations for the game, they are listed under "Another Way to Play."

Perhaps, though, the most important thing you need to know about using this book is what you already know, in your own heart and mind: Play is absolutely essential for children, and any curriculum that excludes it is not meeting the needs of the whole child! I hope, as you play these games with the children, the child who still lives within you comes out to play—and that you have as much fun as the children do!

Circle Games

Circles bring about a sense of community—of belonging—that no other formation offers. Circle times for children have "been around for about a century. Because there is no beginning or end, every individual in a circle is equal and belongs to the whole group" (Butler, 2005, p. 28).

Whether the children are holding hands or simply sitting side by side, the circle is a symbol of togetherness. It allows them to see and hear everyone else. To remain part of the circle, children must accept the rules and roles assigned. Recognition of others and both verbal and nonverbal communication are among the social skills fostered "in the round."

Butler (2005) tells us "the most successful circle times include acceptance, openness, and non-judgmental expression of ideas." Those objectives are certainly part of the games that follow.

This Is My Friend

This game, adapted from Orlick (1982), is a great getting-to-know-you activity for the beginning of the year. And, by modifying it slightly (see "Another Way to Play"), you can use it all year long.

Why It's a Great Game

For cognitive development:
- Developing laterality (understanding that there are two sides to the body)
- Reinforcing the concepts *high* and *around*
- Practicing sequencing

For social/emotional development:
- Learning to cooperate
- Experiencing a feeling of welcome and belonging
- Getting to know one another

For physical development:
- Practicing sequential movement

Themes
Family & Friends

Content Areas
Math
Social Studies

How to Play

Stand in a circle with the children, with everyone holding hands. Raise the hand of the child to your right or left, saying, "This is my friend, _____." That child says his name and raises the arm of the next child in the circle, saying, "This is my friend, _____." The process continues all the way around the circle until all of the children have had a chance to say their names and all arms are in the air. Then, the group takes a big bow!

Another Way to Play

- Once the children know the names of their classmates, they can introduce each other instead of themselves. For example, Michael might raise the arm of the child to his right and say, "This is my friend, Emily."
- When the children are familiar with one another, they can add something of interest about the person they're introducing. For example, Michael might say, "This is my friend Emily, and she likes cats."
- Ask the children what else might they do at the end, instead of taking a bow.

Duck, Duck, Goose

This game appeared in the Physical Education Hall of Shame (see page 9) because, traditionally played, it involves physical activity for only one or two players and a good deal of waiting for the rest of the participants. Also, some players are repeatedly chosen to be the "goose"—sometimes friends of the player who is "IT" or the slowest children, who have little chance of catching IT. And tagged players are relegated to the center of the circle and singled out as "failures." This revised version changes all that!

Why It's a Great Game

For cognitive development:
- Reinforcing the concept *around*
- Learning listening skills

For social/emotional development:
- Creating a sense of belonging
- Developing a sense of humor

For physical development:
- Participating in low- to moderate-intensity physical activity
- Practicing walking in place
- Practicing chasing and fleeing

Content Areas
Language Arts
Math

How to Play

Instead of sitting motionless in a circle, the children stand in a circle and walk in place as the game is played. One child, who is IT, walks around the circle, tapping the other children's shoulders and saying either "duck" or "goose." When he taps someone and says, "Goose!" that person chases IT around the circle, trying to tag him. If she does tag him, he stands in her original place and she gets to be IT. If she doesn't tag him, she returns to her spot and he gets to be IT again. An important ground rule: IT can't choose someone who's already been a "goose" until everyone has had a chance.

Another Way to Play

- Give children the opportunity to practice other locomotor skills performed in place by substituting the walk with a march, bounces, or light jogging.

Cat and Mouse I

The original game has all players, with the exception of the "cat" and the "mouse," simply standing in a circle, and they can be standing there for quite a while, depending on how long it takes the cat to catch the mouse. With two simple modifications, there's more active participation for all!

Why It's a Great Game

For cognitive development:
- Reinforcing the prepositions *around* and *between*

For social/emotional development:
- Creating feelings of belonging
- Leading and following

For physical development:
- Practicing the motor skills of chasing, fleeing, and swaying
- Participating in low- to vigorous-intensity physical activity

Theme
Animals

Content Area
Language Arts

How to Play

Choose two children—one to be the "cat" and one to be the "mouse." The remaining children stand in a circle, slightly apart, and sway side to side. The object of the game is for the cat to catch the mouse on the inside of the circle. However, this is harder than it seems because the mouse can run between two players, who then join hands, keeping the cat from passing through. Time the children, giving each cat one minute (or more, if you feel it works better) to catch the mouse. If the cat can't catch the mouse, the mouse becomes the next cat and another mouse is chosen. If the cat catches the mouse, they both rejoin the circle and a new pair is chosen.

Another Way to Play

- Try playing this fast-paced version: The children in the circle stand and sway with their legs wide apart. The "mouse" has the option of running around the outside of the circle or scooting through the legs of another child into the middle of the circle. If that happens, the player whom the mouse scooted under becomes the cat, and the player who was the mouse takes his place in the circle. The player who was the cat becomes the mouse and has to run away quickly!

Leap Frog

This game is played in the traditional way. It does require a bit of waiting, though, so if you have a large group, divide them into smaller groups.

Why It's a Great Game

For cognitive development:
- Learning about frogs
- Practicing sequencing

For social/emotional development:
- Considering the feelings of others
- Waiting turns

For physical development:
- Practicing jumping

Theme
Animals

Content Areas
Math
Science

How to Play

Ask the children to form a circle, crouched on their hands and feet and facing someone else's back. Designate one child to start as the "frog." That child leaps over the child in front of him, and each succeeding child, by placing his hands on the children's backs for support and straddling his legs as he goes over them. When he returns to his original spot in the circle, the child behind him acts as the frog.

Over & Under

You could play this game in a straight line, but playing it in a circle adds to the feeling of togetherness and better enables the children to see what's going on.

Why It's a Great Game

For cognitive development:
- Reinforcing the prepositions *over, under,* and *through*
- Experiencing the concepts *behind* and *backward*

For social/emotional development:
- Learning to cooperate

For physical development:
- Practicing handling a ball
- Gaining flexibility

Content Areas
Language Arts
Social Studies

How to Play

Materials
Playground ball or small beach ball

The children stand in a circle, each facing the back of another child. Hand the ball to one child, who passes it backward over his head to the next child. The ball goes all the way around the circle in this manner. The children then stand with legs apart and pass the ball behind them, putting the ball between their legs and passing to the next person. When the children are comfortable with both of these ways of passing the ball, have them do it in alternation: one child passing it overhead and the next passing it through the legs.

Name Ball

This simple game is a great way for children to get to know one another's names at the start of the school year. Later, it can be used to impart other pertinent information about each child.

Why It's a Great Game

For cognitive development:
- Reinforcing the concept *around*
- Sequencing

For social/emotional development:
- Getting to know each other

For physical development:
- Practicing tossing and catching

Theme
Family & Friends

Content Areas
Language Arts
Math
Social Studies

How to Play

Materials
A small, easy-to-grip ball

Ask the children to stand in a large circle. One child starts by saying his name and then gently passes the ball to the child to either his right or left, who must then say her name as she catches the ball. The process continues around the circle until all of the children have said their names. Then, to help the children more quickly remember each other's names, reverse the process.

Another Way to Play

- Once the children know each other's names, have them call out the name of the person to whom they're tossing the ball.
- Use this game any time you want the children to share information about themselves. For example, on a Monday you might play the game by having each child who catches the ball offer one sentence about what he did over the weekend.
- For a simplified version, have the children sit with legs straddled. Encourage them to roll the ball across the circle to one another.

Hot Potato

In the traditional version, the child holding the "hot potato" (beanbag or ball) when the music stops is eliminated from the game. But because elimination feels awful and keeps children from practicing their skills, this version keeps everyone participating at some level.

Why It's a Great Game

For cognitive development:
- Reinforcing the concept *around*
- Learning sequencing

For social/emotional development:
- Creating feelings of belonging

For physical development:
- Practicing tossing and catching

Content Areas
Language Arts
Math

How to Play

Materials
2 beanbags (the less challenging option) or small balls
CD or cassette player
Music

As the music plays, the children stand in a large circle and pass the beanbag sequentially around the circle, imagining the beanbag is a hot potato. When the music stops, the child holding the beanbag gives it to the child beside her, steps inside the circle, and is given a second beanbag. As the game/music starts again, the child inside the circle tosses and catches her "hot potato" by herself. When the music stops again and a second child is left holding the beanbag, he also steps inside the circle and the two "insiders" begin tossing their beanbag back and forth to each other. As the game progresses, the game eventually reverses itself, with the children "inside" forming a circle and fewer children "outside" tossing to one another, until there's just one child left in the outer circle.

Movement Mimic

This is similar to the old game of Gossip, where one player begins by whispering something into the ear of the next player, who in turn whispers it to the next player, and so on all the way around the circle. But, here, instead of trying to get the same words all the way around, the children try to replicate the same movement.

Why It's a Great Game

For cognitive development:
- Strengthening observational skills
- Practicing the ability to replicate physically what the eyes see
- Practicing sequencing

For social/emotional development:
- Experiencing feelings of belonging
- Learning to cooperate
- Taking turns

For physical development:
- Practicing a variety of nonlocomotor movements

Content Areas
Art
Math
Social Studies

How to Play

Standing, form a circle with the children and begin by choosing an action that each child must take turns imitating until it comes back to you. For instance, you might gently squeeze the hand of the child to your right, and he must do the same to the child on his right, and so on around the circle (i.e., sequential movement).

Here are some other possible (simple) actions:
- bending the knees and straightening
- jumping once
- hopping once
- lifting and lowering a leg
- bending at the waist and straightening
- raising and lowering arms
- nodding the head

When the children are ready, let them take turns choosing a movement to pass around.

Another Way to Play

- A variation of this game is Make a Face, in which each player must imitate the face made by the previous player. Because the children sit in a circle and there's little movement involved, this is a good warm-up or cool-down game.

The Spokes of the Wheel Go 'Round & 'Round

Ask the children if they have seen the spokes on a bicycle wheel. Talk to them about the concept before starting this game.

Why It's a Great Game

For cognitive development:

- Reinforcing the concept *around*

For social/emotional development:
- Learning to cooperate
- Learning about teamwork
- Experiencing feelings of belonging

For physical development:
- Increasing spatial awareness
- Practicing walking and turning at the same time

Theme
Transportation

Content Areas
Language Arts
Math
Social Studies

How to Play

Ask the children to stand in a close circle, each child facing someone else's back. The children then extend their arms toward the inside of the circle so everyone's hands are touching. They then go 'round and 'round, like a bicycle wheel, trying to keep all the spokes attached!

Another Way to Play

- When the children are comfortable with this, try gradually increasing the speed at which the "wheel" turns. The faster it goes, the more fun they'll have!

Do as I Say

This game requires concentration! Start off slowly—speak slowly and give just a few commands at a time. Even if you notice children aren't getting it quite right, just smile and move right along to the next challenge.

Why It's a Great Game

For cognitive development:
- Improving listening skills
- Improving sequential memory
- Following directions

For social/emotional development:
- Increasing feelings of belonging

For physical development:
- Practicing a variety of movements

Content Area
Language Arts

How to Play

The children stand in a circle, with you in the center. Explain that you're going to give them a short list of things to do but that they're not to do them until you've completed the list. Then present such challenges as:
- Jump forward, jump backward.
- Clap twice, blink your eyes.
- Turn yourself around, give yourself a hug.
- Touch your knees, touch your head.
- Clap twice, blink your eyes, turn around.

Another Way to Play

- With older, more experienced children, you can extend the list of commands even further. They may not be able to "clap twice, blink eyes, turn around, give yourself a hug," but they'll have fun trying!

Punchinello

This game offers a wonderful opportunity for children to think back over learning experiences and to reinforce them. If time permits, let every child have a chance to be Punchinello. Another possibility is to assign one or two Punchinellos per day.

Why It's a Great Game

For cognitive development:
- Learning to solve problems
- Reviewing learning experiences
- Learning about rhyming

For social/emotional development:
- Increasing self-awareness

For physical development:
- Practicing a variety of movements

Content Area
Language Arts

How to Play

The children form a circle, with one child in the center who is "Punchinello." The children chant, "What can you do, Punchinello, funny fellow? What can you do, Punchinello, funny you?" The child in the center chooses a movement skill or other learning experience from that day or week to demonstrate (for example, making a geometric shape, or performing the actions of a character from a story). The rest of the children chant, "We can do it, too, Punchinello, funny fellow! We can do it, too, Punchinello, funny you!" Then, they imitate the actions of the child in the center of the circle.

Hoops I

Although this game could be played easily with the hoops in a scattered formation—and you may choose to do that sometimes—playing it in a circle has more of a "community" feel and means that all of the children are leading and following.

Why It's a Great Game

For cognitive development:
- Reinforcing the concepts *around*, *next*, and *inside of*

For social/emotional development:
- Creating feelings of belonging
- Leading and following

For physical development:
- Practicing jumping, leaping, and/or hopping
- Performing moderate-intensity exercise

Content Areas
Language Arts
Math
Social Studies

How to Play

Materials
1 plastic hoop per child

Arrange the hoops in a circle and place them close enough so that they are touching. Each child stands inside a hoop. At your signal, they begin jumping (two-footed push-offs and landings) around the circle, from inside one hoop to inside the next.

Another Way to Play

- When the children are adept at jumping from hoop to hoop, challenge them to try leaping (one leg extended to the front and the other to the back) from hoop to hoop.
- When they have enough balance to be successful at it, invite them to hop from hoop to hoop. They'll first try it on the dominant foot, but after some practice, encourage them to try the non-dominant one.

Rotate It I

This is the first of several games involving a parachute. Being in a circle with everyone else is always enjoyable to children, but playing in a circle around a colorful parachute makes the experience even more magical! This is an excellent introductory activity that familiarizes the children with gripping the parachute.

Why It's a Great Game

For cognitive development:
- Experiencing the concept *rotation*

For social/emotional development:
- Learning to cooperate

For physical development:
- Practicing gripping and handing off

Content Areas
Music
Science
Social Studies

How to Play

Materials
Parachute

The children stand around the parachute. Then, remaining in place, they rotate it by passing it to the right or left. Be sure to rotate it in both directions!

Another Way to Play

- As the children rotate the parachute, they can sing the following song to the tune of "Here We Go 'Round the Mulberry Bush":

    This is the way we move the chute,
    Move the chute, move the chute.
    This is the way we move the chute.
    Here at [name of center or school].

- When the children have enough experience gripping and passing the parachute, time the activity by asking them to see how many full rotations they can accomplish in one minute, for example.

Rotate It II

In this version of Rotate It (see Rotate It I on page 26), the children rotate with the parachute. If they're cognitively ready to accept the problem-solving challenge, rather than telling them how to do it, ask them to find three different ways to move the chute around while holding it with one hand, for example.

Why It's a Great Game

For cognitive development:
- Reinforcing the concepts *rotation* and *around*

For social/emotional development:
- Learning to cooperate
- Creating feelings of belonging

For physical development:
- Practicing a variety of locomotor skills
- Peforming moderate-intensity physical activity

Content Areas
Science
Social Studies

How to Play

Materials
Parachute

Holding the parachute with one hand, at waist height, the children walk in a circle, first in one direction and then the other. They can also try rotating it by tiptoeing, marching, galloping, jumping, and hopping.

Another Way to Play

- More difficult is moving in one direction while facing another (such as walking backwards). When the children are ready, invite them to hold the parachute with two hands, facing it, and rotate it while sliding to the side (one foot leads and the other plays catch-up).
- With any of these activities the children can accompany their movements with a song sung to "Here We Go 'Round the Mulberry Bush." For example:

    Here we go 'round the parachute,
    The parachute, the parachute.
    Here we go 'round the parachute.
    Here at [name of center or school].

Making Waves

Discuss waves with the children before playing this game. Have they been to the ocean? Do they know what a ripple is? How much difference is there between a ripple and a wave?

Why It's a Great Game

For cognitive development:
- Learning about ocean waves
- Experiencing the continuum from small to large

For social/emotional development:
- Learning to cooperate
- Learning about teamwork
- Experiencing feelings of belonging

For physical development:
- Exercising the upper torso

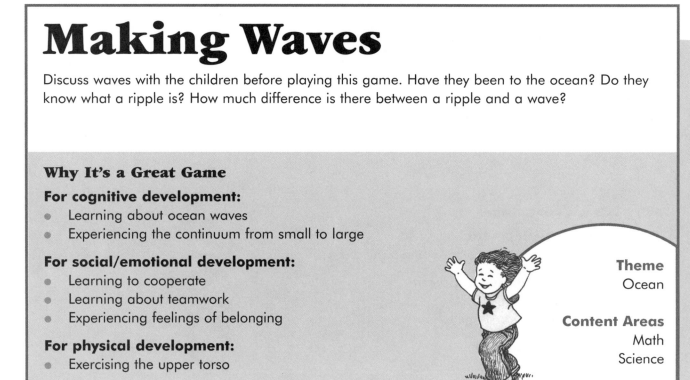

Theme
Ocean

Content Areas
Math
Science

How to Play

Materials
Parachute

Standing around the parachute, the children start by making small up-and-down hand motions that cause little ripples. Gradually, the ripples (hand and arm movements) get larger and larger, until they are gigantic ocean waves.

Another Way to Play

- Encourage the children to experiment with making ripples and waves while kneeling and sitting. Which is easiest? Which is hardest?
- Invite the children to try alternating movements (for example, one child raises his arms as the next lowers hers, and so on around the circle).
- Challenge the group to make ripples and waves by moving their own arms up and down in opposition (one hand going up and the other coming down).

Let It Snow

Simply moving the parachute up and down can be fun, but this game sustains children's interest and adds cognitive elements.

Why It's a Great Game

For cognitive development:
- Learning about snow and seasons
- Counting

For social/emotional development:
- Learning to cooperate
- Learning about teamwork

For physical development:
- Exercising upper torso muscles
- Practicing visual tracking

Theme
Seasons

Content Areas
Math
Science
Social Studies

How to Play

Materials
Parachute
Cotton balls or Styrofoam peanuts

Place the cotton balls or peanuts on the parachute. Ask the children to form a circle around the parachute. Next, encourage the children to lift the parachute carefully. Challenge them to move it up and down in little waves, creating a "snowstorm" and working together to keep all the "flakes" from falling off the parachute. Ask them to count the number of times they can move the parachute up and down without any of the snowflakes falling off. (You might want to give them a set time period, marking the beginning and end with a signal.) Gradually, challenge them to toss the snowflakes higher while still keeping them on the parachute.

Another Way to Play

- You can turn this into a seasonal game by using items like fallen leaves in autumn, a small beach ball in the summer, and flower petals in the spring.
- Play the game in the opposite way—see how quickly they can shake the objects off the parachute!

Going Up!

Talk to the children about elevators. Have they ever been in one?

Why It's a Great Game

For cognitive development:
- Reinforcing the concepts *up* and *down*
- Learning about elevators

For social/emotional development:
- Learning to cooperate

For physical development:
- Exercising the lower and upper torso
- Experiencing moving through the three levels (low, middle, and high) in space

Content Areas
Math
Science

How to Play

Materials
Parachute

Pretend the parachute is an elevator. Begin with it at "ground level" and then slowly move up the "floors," until it has reached the highest level it can! The elevator must then go back down. You can vary the speed at which the elevator travels and even include stops. How still can the "elevator" stay while stopped?

Body Buddy

Identifying various body parts, as children do in games like Simon Says (see page 39), can be fun, but moving a parachute in front of body parts adds a whole new dimension.

Why It's a Great Game

For cognitive development:
- Identifying body parts
- Developing listening skills

For social/emotional development:
- Learning to cooperate

For physical development:
- Increasing flexibility
- Practicing moving through the levels (low, middle, and high) in space

Theme
My Body

Content Areas
Language Arts
Science

How to Play

Materials
Parachute

Challenge the children to move and hold the chute in front of various body parts. Start slowly, but as children become adept at this, move more quickly from one position to the next! Possible parts include:
- tummy
- chest
- knees
- ankles
- toes
- forehead
- shoulders
- neck
- hips
- shins

Parachute Lady (Guy) Says

This game is played like Simon Says (see page 39) but with a parachute and without elimination.

Why It's a Great Game

For cognitive development:
- Improving listening skills
- Practicing following directions

For social/emotional development:
- Learning about teamwork
- Experiencing feelings of togetherness

For physical development:
- Improving flexibility
- Performing low-intensity exercise for the whole body
- Experiencing moving through low, middle, and high levels in space

Content Areas
Language Arts
Social Studies

How to Play

Materials
Parachute

The children face the parachute and hold it with both hands. Issue commands, beginning each sentence with "Parachute Lady [Guy] says…"
- Shake the parachute.
- Freeze!
- Raise the chute high.
- Lower the chute to the floor.
- Make waves.
- Bring the chute to your knees (head, shoulders, tummy, etc.).
- Make ripples.
- Walk toward the center.
- Walk back out.
- Make the parachute fly!

The Igloo

As simple as this seems, the children will want to do it again and again! As adults, we just have to remember how valuable repetition is to young children.

Why It's a Great Game

For cognitive development:
- Reinforcing the concepts *low* and *high*
- Experimenting with inflation and deflation

For social/emotional development:
- Learning to cooperate
- Experiencing feelings of belonging

For physical development:
- Exercising the upper and lower torso
- Practicing moving through the three levels (low, middle, and high) in space

Theme
Homes & Habitats

Content Areas
Science
Social Studies

How to Play

Materials
Parachute

The children start by holding the parachute close to the floor. They then raise it, eventually reaching as high into the air as possible, and pull it quickly back down, trapping air under the chute.

Another Way to Play

Encourage the children to:
- lie down as the parachute is lowered, hands under the parachute and bodies on the outside.
- hold the parachute with crossed hands, turning to face the outside as the parachute is lowered. This places them inside the "igloo" when the chute is brought to the floor.
- let go of the chute when it reaches its highest point.

Light as a Feather

Although the children could be divided into teams that compete with each other to blow the feather off the parachute, a cooperative version offers the children a great deal more.

Why It's a Great Game

For cognitive development:
- Experiencing the concepts *light* and *flotation*

For social/emotional development:
- Learning to cooperate
- Learning about teamwork

For physical development:
- Improving lung capacity

Content Areas
Science
Social Studies

How to Play

Materials
Parachute
A feather

The children sit in a circle around a parachute and lift it to chin level. Place a feather in the center of the parachute and challenge the children to work together to blow it off!

Roll Around

This challenging activity requires both concentration and patience.

Why It's a Great Game

For cognitive development:
- Experiencing the concepts *around* and *outer edge*
- Improving concentration

For social/emotional development:
- Learning to cooperate
- Learning about teamwork

For physical development:
- Exercising the upper torso
- Practicing eye-hand coordination

Content Areas
Language Arts
Math
Social Studies

How to Play

Materials
Parachute
Small ball

Place a ball on the parachute. Everyone then works together to try to get it to roll around the outer edge—first in one direction and then the other.

Hole in One

This challenging activity should only be attempted after the children have much experience playing with the parachute.

Why It's a Great Game

For cognitive development:
- Reinforcing the concept *through*

For social/emotional development:
- Learning about teamwork
- Learning to cooperate

For physical development:
- Exercising the upper torso
- Practicing eye-hand coordination

Content Areas
Language Arts
Social Studies

How to Play

Materials
Parachute
A ball smaller than the hole in the center of the chute

Place the ball on the parachute. Everyone then works together to try to get it through the hole in the middle.

Concept Games

Traditionally, we've associated playing games with improving children's physical development. While actively playing, children often use their large muscles. As they chase, flee, and dodge they expend large amounts of energy, which burns calories and builds muscle strength and endurance. Thus, the association with physical development is a natural one.

However, children also learn a great deal from the games they play. Some of the skills they learn—following rules, taking turns, and communicating—fall under the heading of social development. But playing games promotes cognitive and brain development, as well. Anyone who spends time around young children knows that they learn best when they experience concepts. As Rui Olds (1994) explains, "Between birth and five or six years, children's bodies, as much as their minds, are the organs of intelligence." Furthermore, energetic activities such as chasing, fleeing, and dodging "feed" the brain with oxygen and glucose, helping to optimize the brain's performance. Thanks to advances in research, we now know that most of the brain is activated during physical activity—much more so than when doing sedentary tasks.

The games in this chapter tend to focus on a few particular concepts. These games will help imprint those concepts on both the bodies and minds of children as they play.

Heads, Shoulders, Knees, and Toes

This body-part identification game requires children to listen carefully as they move from body part to body part. **Note:** Children are extremely flexible but they should still keep knees slightly bent when they reach down to touch their toes.

Why It's a Great Game

For cognitive development:
- Identifying body parts
- Improving listening skills

For social/emotional development:
- Increasing self-awareness

For physical development:
- Practicing bending and straightening
- Improving flexibility

Theme
My Body

Content Areas
Language Arts
Music
Social Studies

How to Play

As you call out "head," "shoulders," "knees," and "toes," children touch the corresponding part of their bodies. First, follow the order of the title, and then mix it up!

Head, Shoulders, Knees, and Toes

Head, shoulders, knees, and toes,
Knees and toes.
Head, shoulders, knees, and toes,
Knees and toes.

And eyes and ears and mouth and nose,
Head, shoulders, knees, and toes,
Knees and toes!

Another Way to Play

- Change the tempo at which you call out the body parts, sometimes doing it slowly and sometimes quickly. You can also start very slowly and gradually increase the tempo until the children dissolve into fits of giggles!
- Substitute a sound for the word "head" (for example, a hand clap, a click of the tongue, a foot stomp, or a kissing sound). Tell the children to touch their heads when they hear that sound. With each successive verse, substitute a different sound for one more body part, until you've replaced all four parts with four different sounds.
- Do any of the above while chanting or singing the song of the same title, which incorporates additional body parts.

Simon Says

In the traditional game, those children who need the most practice with either listening skills or identifying body parts often are the first to be eliminated! You can promote the skill development and enjoyment of all the children by playing this game without the elimination process.

Why It's a Great Game

For cognitive development:
- Improving listening skills
- Identifying body parts

For social/emotional development:
- Improving self-concept

For physical development:
- Practicing a variety of nonlocomotor movements

Theme
My Body

Content Areas
Language Arts
Science

How to Play

Organize the children into two groups (forming two lines or two circles). Explain that they should do as you say only when the command is preceded by the words "Simon says." Then, issue commands like the ones below, sometimes saying, "Simon says," and sometimes not. **Note:** For new (very young) players, say "Simon Says" before every challenge. If a child moves without Simon's "permission," that child simply relocates from one line or circle to the other. "Simon" might make requests like the following:

- Raise your arms.
- Touch your toes.
- Wiggle your nose.
- Bend and touch your knees.
- Make a funny face.
- Touch your head.
- Touch your shoulders.
- Stand on one foot.
- Blink your eyes.
- Give yourself a hug!
- Stand up tall.
- Pucker up your lips.
- Put hands on hips.
- Reach for the sky.

Another Way to Play

- As children become more adept at this game, increase the challenge by increasing the tempo at which you call out the challenges. Expect lots of giggles!

Follow the Leader

This traditional game is so simple to play it may seem impossible that it could teach so much. But the list of benefits below proves that sometimes simpler is better!

Why It's a Great Game

For cognitive development:
- Improving observational skills
- Physically imitating what the eyes see
- Following directions

For social/emotional development:
- Learning to cooperate
- Practicing following and leading
- Learning about sharing space

For physical development:
- Improving a variety of movement skills
- Practicing with different pathways (straight, curving, and zigzagging), levels, body shapes, and tempos

Content Areas
Art
Social Studies

How to Play

Lead the children in a line around the room, varying the locomotor skills you use (walking, jogging, tiptoeing, galloping) and the pathways you move along (straight, curving, and zigzagging).

Another Way to Play

- Once the children are comfortable with this game, you can add more variety to your movements, changing their level in space (high, low, mid-range), pace (slow, fast), and force (light, strong), as well as your body's shape. Also, pause occasionally to perform a nonlocomotor skill (bending, stretching, twisting, and so forth).
- When the children are ready for the responsibility, let them take turns leading.

Choo-Choo

Talk to the children about trains, and how trains are made up of individual "cars."

Why It's a Great Game

For cognitive development:
- Learning about trains

For social/emotional development:
- Learning to cooperate
- Practicing following and leading
- Experiencing feelings of togetherness

For physical development:
- Performing moderate-intensity physical activity
- Practicing different pathways (straight, curving, and zigzagging), directions, and tempos

Theme
Transportation

Content Area
Social Studies

How to Play

The children form a line behind you, placing their hands on the hips, waist, or shoulders of the child in front of them. Then, calling out "choo-choo," the "train" chugs along, gradually picking up speed. The goal is to stay connected. But if one of the "cars" disconnects, that car forms another train with the cars behind her.

Me and My Shadow

Children play this game in pairs. One child stands with his back to the second child.

Why It's a Great Game

For cognitive development:
- Improving observational skills
- Physically replicating what the eyes see
- Reinforcing the positional concepts *front* and *back*
- Learning about shadows

For social/emotional development:
- Learning to cooperate
- Learning about accepting others' ideas
- Learning to lead and follow
- Practicing taking turns

For physical development:
- Practicing a variety of locomotor and nonlocomotor skills

Content Areas
Art
Science
Social Studies

How to Play

The child in front performs various movements, both in place and traveling, and the child in back imitates the movements, or "shadows" the child in front. At your signal, the children switch roles.

Home Base

This game borrows elements from both Musical Chairs (see page 73) and Follow the Leader (see page 40). Although the children will love the suspense of waiting to see who's next to follow you, choose the children rather quickly so that no child spends too much time sitting.

Why It's a Great Game

For cognitive development:
- Learning observational skills
- Practicing listening skills
- Imitating physically what the eyes see

For social/emotional development:
- Practicing safely sharing space

For physical development:
- Practicing a variety of locomotor skills
- Performing moderate- to vigorous-intensity physical activity

Content Areas
Art
Language Arts
Social Studies

How to Play

Materials
1 chair per child
Rhythm sticks

Line up the chairs, alternating the way they face (that is, the first faces the east or north wall, the second faces the west or south wall, and so forth). The children each sit in a chair, which is their "home base." Walk around the chairs, carrying the rhythm sticks and stopping periodically to tap a child on the knee with one. That child then stands up and follows you, mimicking all of your movements, as you continue to move around the chairs. Eventually all of the children will be following you and mimicking your actions. At some point, tap the rhythm sticks together twice. This is the children's signal to try to get back to their home bases as quickly as possible. The hitch is that you're going to take a seat, too. The child whose seat you take gets the rhythm sticks for the next round.

Fast Firefighters

Takes Time

The children may want to play this game over and over again, just for the fun and excitement of it. Following the last round, you can invite them to explore other aspects of being a firefighter. For example, they could pretend to run to the truck, drive to the fire, and put it out.

Why It's a Great Game

For cognitive development:
- Learning about the occupation of firefighting
- Reinforcing the concept *quickly*

For social/emotional development:
- Experiencing feelings of belonging
- Developing a sense of humor

For physical development:
- Performing moderate- to vigorous-intensity physical activity
- Developing coordination

Theme
Occupations

Content Areas
Language Arts
Social Studies

How to Play

Materials
One chair per child
The children's jackets

Turn the children's jackets inside out (you can have them help you with this). Then line up the chairs. Depending on the number of chairs/children there are, you can put them either in one line or two, with about two feet between them. (If you choose to have two lines, set up the chairs so they're facing each other but with enough space between them so the children can maneuver without bumping into each other.) Place one inside-out jacket on the back of each chair. The child whose jacket is on it sits on the chair. The children close their eyes and pretend to be firefighters sleeping at the station. At your signal (which should sound like a fire bell), the "firefighters" jump up from their chairs, run around to the backs of them, and race to turn their jackets inside-right and put them on!

Touch It!

Play this game indoors or out.

Why It's a Great Game

For cognitive development:
- Improving listening skills
- Learning to identify colors

For social/emotional development:
- Experiencing feelings of belonging
- Practicing sharing space

For physical development:
- Learning about spatial awareness
- Performing low- to moderate-level physical activity

Content Areas
Art
Language Arts

How to Play

With the children scattered about the room or outside area, call out, "Touch red!" The children then run to touch something red, whether it's an object or on someone else's clothing. Continue with as many colors as you can see.

Another Way to Play

- You can do the same thing with shapes ("Touch something round!"), textures (smooth, rough, hard, soft, etc.), or objects ("Touch a tree trunk!" "Touch a blade of grass!" "Touch a wall!").

Traffic Lights

Before beginning, talk to the children about traffic lights and explain what each color means.

Why It's a Great Game

For cognitive development:
- Learning about traffic safety
- Learning color discrimination

For social/emotional development:
- Practicing how to safely share a space

For physical development:
- Practicing stopping and starting
- Practicing the movement element of flow (moving in uninterrupted or interrupted ways)
- Practicing a variety of locomotor skills
- Experiencing a variety of pathways through space (straight, curving, or zigzagging)

Theme
Transportation

Content Areas
Art
Social Studies

How to Play

Materials

Three large pieces of paper: one green, one yellow, and one red

Hold up the green paper and invite the children to walk around the room, pretending that they're driving cars. When you hold up the yellow paper, they walk in place. When you hold up red, they come to a complete stop. Only the green paper can get them "driving" around the room again.

Another Way to Play

- You can use this game as an opportunity to practice a variety of movement skills. Once the children are familiar with the game, change the walk to any other locomotor skill (for example, galloping or skipping) that they're all capable of performing.

Red Light, Green Light

In the traditional version of this game, children who fail to stop when they are supposed to are singled out to start all over again. In addition, there is one winner and the rest of the children lose. With a slight modification, the game involves more physical activity, more learning concepts, and more fun!

Why It's a Great Game

For cognitive development:
- Developing listening skills
- Reinforcing the concepts *stop* and go
- Reinforcing traffic safety rules

For social/emotional development:
- Improving self-control

For physical development:
- Practicing stopping and starting on signal
- Experiencing the movement element of flow (moving in interrupted or uninterrupted ways)

Theme
Transportation

Content Areas
Art
Social Studies

How to Play

Ask the children to line up side by side. Acting as the "stoplight," stand a distance from the children with your back to them. When the stoplight says, "Green light," the children run or tiptoe toward you. When the stoplight suddenly turns and says "Red light," everyone must stop and hold very still. If you see players who haven't been able to stop in time, designate them to be "yellow lights," which means they must walk in place until the signal to go is given again. When someone finally reaches the stoplight, the game starts all over again with someone else acting as stoplight (you can decide in advance the number and order of the children who will get to be stoplights).

The Tightrope

With this game, children won't know they are practicing their balancing skills and gaining experience with the directions *forward, backward,* and *sideways.* They will only know they're having fun pretending to be in the circus.

Why It's a Great Game

For cognitive development:
- Learning about direction
- Stimulating the imagination

For social/emotional development
- Increasing self-confidence
- Developing a sense of humor

For physical development:
- Learning to balance
- Improving spatial awareness

Theme
The Circus

Content Areas
Language Arts
Math
Social Studies

How to Play

Materials
Several long jump ropes (to keep children from waiting too long for a turn)

Place the ropes in straight lines on the floor or ground. Then invite the children to pretend they're walking the tightropes like acrobats in the circus. Once the children are comfortable walking in a forward direction, invite them to try to walk sideways in both directions and, finally, backward.

Another Way to Play
- The next step is for the children to try different locomotor skills. You can either assign different skills—such as tiptoeing, galloping, and hopping—or add a problem-solving element to the activity. For example, challenge them to find three different ways to move across the tightrope in a forward direction.

Sleeping Giants

This game couldn't be simpler. That's probably why children love it.

Why It's a Great Game

For cognitive development:
- Improving listening skills
- Following directions

For social/emotional development:
- Feeling a sense of belonging
- Developing a sense of humor

For physical development:
- Practicing jumping
- Performing moderate- to vigorous-intensity physical activity
- Practicing stopping and starting
- Building muscular strength and endurance

Theme
Creatures &
Critters

Content Area
Language Arts

How to Play

The children jump up and down until you call out, "Sleeping giants!" Then, they collapse to the floor and lie very still. When you call out, "Waking giants!" the children start jumping again.

Another Way to Play

- Substitute other motor skills instead of jumping.

Number Ball

Children enjoy this simple game so much they won't even notice they are working on their counting skills.

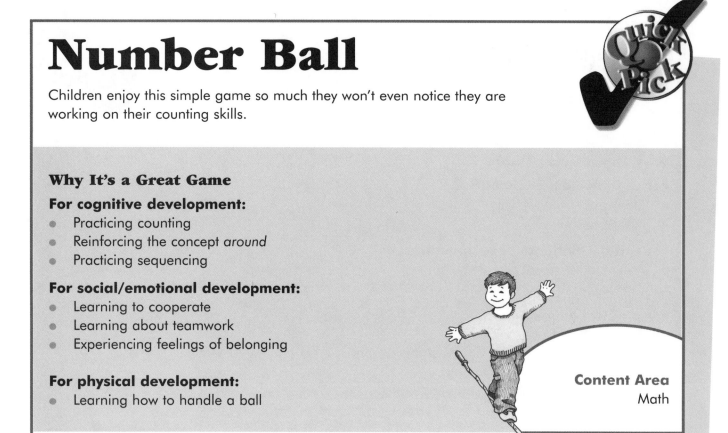

Why It's a Great Game

For cognitive development:
- Practicing counting
- Reinforcing the concept *around*
- Practicing sequencing

For social/emotional development:
- Learning to cooperate
- Learning about teamwork
- Experiencing feelings of belonging

For physical development:
- Learning how to handle a ball

Content Area
Math

How to Play

Materials
Playground ball or small beach ball

The children stand in a circle and pass a ball around. The first child counts, "One" out loud, and as the children pass the ball to the next person, they say the next consecutive number.

Another Way to Play

- When the children know the alphabet well enough, they can play the game practicing their letters.

Find the Farm Animals

This fun game allows children a chance to use their imaginations and feel empathy for animals that are lost and can't find their way home. Before you play, you'll need to hide the animals throughout the classroom.

Why It's a Great Game

For cognitive development:
- Improving visual discrimination

For social/emotional development:
- Pretending
- Developing empathy

For physical development:
- Practicing moving at a low level in space (near the floor)

Theme
Animals

Content Areas
Art
Science
Social Studies

How to Play

Materials
Stuffed or plastic animals representing animals found on a farm

Designate a spot in the classroom as the barn. Then, pretending to be farmers, the children search for all their lost animals, bringing them back to the barn as they find them.

Another Way to Play

- Depending on what is available, offer the children similar experiences with other animals, such as lost pets or jungle animals!
- Do this kind of "treasure hunt" with any objects the children will enjoy finding—indoors or out!

Through the Hoop

If the groups are small, there will be less waiting time for all involved. Also, by scattering single-file lines of children throughout the room, rather than placing them side by side, the children will be less inclined to see this as a race.

Why It's a Great Game

For cognitive development:
- Reinforcing the concept *through*

For social/emotional development:
- Learning about teamwork
- Experiencing feelings of belonging

For physical development:
- Performing moderate- to vigorous-intensity physical activity
- Improving coordination

Content Areas
Language Arts
Social Studies

How to Play

Materials
1 plastic hoop per 4 to 5 children

Give the first child in each single-file line a hoop and demonstrate how to hold it upright. The object is for each child to get through the hoop while holding it and then pass it to the next child. Once through the hoop, a player goes to the end of the line.
If you make this a timed activity, during which the children must see how many times they can get through the hoop, it will get their hearts pumping—and children laughing— even harder!

Belly Laughs

Young children love to be silly, and this hysterical game will crack them up!

Why It's a Great Game

For cognitive development:
- Learning about sequencing

For social/emotional development:
- Experiencing feelings of belonging
- Developing a sense of humor

For physical development:
- Exercising abdominal muscles

Content Areas
Math
Social Studies

How to Play

Ask the children to lie on their backs and place their heads on the belly of the child next to them. (You may have to help with this arrangement!) Point to one child, who says, "Ha!" The child whose head is on that child's belly must then say, "Ha-ha!" The third child says, "Ha-ha-ha," and so on, down the line until each child has contributed a "ha" to the process and everyone is giggling.

Kangaroo!

Young children won't mind that you're making the task of jumping harder than usual because they will be having so much fun.

Why It's a Great Game

For cognitive development:
- Reinforcing the concepts *up*, *down*, and *forward*

For social/emotional development:
- Experiencing feelings of belonging
- Enjoying humor

For physical development:
- Jumping
- Practicing moving with limitations
- Performing moderate- to vigorous-intensity physical activity
- Building muscular strength and endurance

Content Areas
Language Arts
Math

How to Play

Materials
1 small ball per child

Designate a starting and ending point, and ask children to move from one to the other. The only thing is, to get there they have to jump while holding a ball between their knees! If they drop the ball, they just pick it up, put it back between their knees, and start jumping again.

Another Way to Play

- Encourage the children to try this as they walk from the starting point to the ending point.

Shrinking Room

When children share general space without an understanding that they each carry their own personal space with them, chaos can result. In fact, for young children it's often more fun to "crash and go boom" than to avoid interfering with one another's movements. This game can change all that!

Why It's a Great Game

For cognitive development:
- Solving problems

For social/emotional development:
- Respecting others' personal space
- Moving safely through shared space

For physical development:
- Experiencing moving along a variety of pathways

Content Area
Social Studies

How to Play

Materials
1 hoop per child

Ask each child to step inside a hoop, pick it up, and put it around his waist. Then challenge the children to imagine they're each inside either giant bubbles or cars on the highway (whichever image you think will work best with your group). Challenge them to move around the room without touching anyone else's bubble or car. Stand with your arms out to your sides, acting as a "wall," beyond which they can't pass. Gradually, begin reducing the size of the area in which the children have to move. Be sure to stop while the children are still able to move around without touching another person's hoop!

Another Way to Play

- If you don't have hoops, the children can still play this game by extending their arms out to their sides. In this case, instead of avoiding contact with other hoops, they'll be avoiding contact with other hands.

Match That Shape

In its own way, this game offers children the opportunity to consider the differences and similarities among people. If they get stuck for ideas, you can encourage them by suggesting they try using different body parts and levels in space.

Why It's a Great Game

For cognitive development:
- Replicating physically what the eyes see
- Improving observational skills

For social/emotional development:
- Learning to cooperate

For physical development:
- Experiencing the movement element of shape (the different shapes the body can assume)

Theme
Shapes

Content Areas
Art
Math

How to Play

Children choose partners and determine who is "A" and who is "B." At a signal from you, A moves to a different part of the room and creates a body shape of her choosing. A holds this position until B joins her and, facing her, assumes the same shape (like a mirror image). Once this has been done, B goes off to form a different shape, which A must then match.

Alphabet Shapes

Imitating the straight and curving lines of the letters of the alphabet helps children imprint their form and directionality on their bodies and in their minds. Doing it with one another makes it a game and, therefore, relieves any anxiety they may feel about letter recognition.

Why It's a Great Game

For cognitive development:
- Learning the letters of the alphabet
- Exploring straight and curving lines

For social/emotional development:
- Learning to cooperate
- Learning about teamwork

For physical development:
- Learning about spatial awareness
- Exploring straight and curving body shapes

Content Areas
Art
Language Arts
Social Studies

How to Play

Materials
The alphabet, posted for children to see

Divide the children into groups of three and four. Call out a letter, pointing to where it is posted. Each group then works together to make the shape of that letter.

Thunder and Lightning

Talk to the children about thunder and lightning. Do they know that thunder is the sound that follows lightning?

Why It's a Great Game

For cognitive development:
- Exploring weather concepts

For social/emotional development:
- Learning to cooperate
- Gaining experience with leading and following
- Learning self-expression

For physical development:
- Performing moderate-intensity physical activity

Theme
Weather

Content Areas
Science
Social Studies

How to Play

Children choose partners and then decide who will be "lightning" and who will be "thunder." (They will get to be both eventually.) When you give the signal to go, the children separate from one another and move around the room, keeping their eyes on each other the whole time. When the child acting as lightning "strikes" (moves in the way she thinks lightning moves), "thunder" responds by moving in the way she thinks thunder does. When they are ready, encourage the children to switch roles.

Bread and Butter

Talk to the children about bread—toasted or plain—and butter before starting this game.

Why It's a Great Game

For cognitive development:
- Developing listening skills
- Following directions

For social/emotional development:
- Learning to cooperate
- Enjoying togetherness
- Experiencing positive physical contact

For physical development:
- Practicing a variety of locomotor skills

Content Area
Social Studies

How to Play

Whisper the words "bread" or "butter" into the ear of each child (try to have an even number of each). Then, give the children a signal to start walking around the room. When they come face to face with another player, the two children say their assigned roles. If one says "bread" and the other "butter," they hug (blending the two) and then go on their way. If both children say the same word, they just move along. The goal is to "butter" as much bread as possible before you give the signal to stop.

Another Way to Play

- Once the children are familiar with this game, ask them to move around the room using other locomotor skills, such as tiptoeing, jogging, or skipping.
- You can make this a game of Salt and Pepper in which the children shake hands when they come face to face with their opposite.

Sitting in the Dark

This game is best played by children with plenty of previous experience moving in both personal and general space.

Why It's a Great Game

For cognitive development:
- Improving listening skills
- Learning to follow directions

For social/emotional development:
- Empathizing with the visually impaired

For physical development:
- Increasing spatial awareness

Content Areas
Language Arts
Social Studies

How to Play

Materials
1 chair per child

Arrange the chairs in a circle, facing outward, or in one or two lines (facing in opposite directions), with at least 12" of space between chairs. Ask the children to stand in front of a chair and close their eyes. Then, issue directions such as, "Take three steps forward," or "Take two jumps forward." The children do as directed and then reverse the process—without opening their eyes or turning around—and try to get back to their chairs and sit down.

Another Way to Play

- If there is enough space between the chairs—and the children know right and left—include sideways movements in your instructions. For example, ask them to take two steps to the right, or one hop to the left.

Musical Games

Wherever there are children, there is music. Music is mood altering, soothing, amusing, or energizing. Children love to sing, move to music, and make up their own sounds and songs, from the silly to the profound. They progress from creating their own rhythms to moving as one with an imposed rhythm. A song played over and over again becomes as comforting and familiar to them as a favorite stuffed animal.

Music also contributes to the development of the cognitive domain. It is vital to the development of language and listening skills (Pica, 2004). Music and language arts both consist of symbols and, when used in combination, abstract concepts become more concrete. Music also helps expand vocabulary and improve attention and memory. (Is there anyone who learned their ABCs without benefit of the alphabet song?)

Songs, movement, and musical games are "brilliant neurological exercises" vital to intellectual development. By combining rhythmic movement with speech and song, young children are being given an opportunity to further develop their minds, particularly in the areas of "inner speech" and "impulse control," which contribute to language development, selflmanagement, and social skills (Coulter, 1995, p. 22).

Ring Around the Rosie

This traditional game is developmentally appropriate in its original form.

Why It's a Great Game

For cognitive development:
- Reinforcing the concepts *up, down,* and *around*
- Experiencing rhyme

For social/emotional development:
- Experiencing a sense of belonging

For physical development:
- Developing spatial awareness
- Performing low-intensity exercise

Content Areas
Language Arts
Math
Music

How to Play

Standing in a circle and holding hands, the children sing the following lines, falling to the floor on the last line. Then they get up and do it again!

Ring Around the Rosie
Ring around the rosie,
Pocket full of posies,
Ashes, ashes,
We all fall down!

Another Way to Play

- Change the tempo of the song as you go along and children will explore the musical element of *tempo* and the movement element of *time,* and they will have even more fun! Start by singing it very, very slowly. Then, with every repetition of the game, sing it a little faster.
- Play this game with a parachute. The children hold the chute with one hand and walk in a circle on the first two lines. On "ashes, ashes," they stop and wave the chute up and down twice. And, of course, on the last line, they all fall down!

London Bridge Is Falling Down

The traditional version of this game is mostly sedentary for the children who act as the bridge and for those subsequent children who are "captured." With a slight modification, the children can move almost continually.

Why It's a Great Game

For cognitive development:
- Reinforcing concepts *through* and *under*

For social/emotional development:
- Creating feelings of belonging
- Taking turns

For physical development:
- Practicing various locomotor skills
- Performing low-intensity exercise

Content Areas
Language Arts
Math
Music

How to Play

Select two children to stand facing each other, hands linked and arms raised, creating the "bridge." The rest of the children form a single-file line, and as they move under the bridge, everybody sings the song. Make sure everyone gets a chance to make the bridge.

London Bridge Is Falling Down

London Bridge is falling down,
Falling down, falling down.
London Bridge is falling down,
My fair lady.

Build it up with iron bars,
Iron bars, iron bars,
Build it up with iron bars,
My fair lady.

Iron bars will bend and break,
Bend and break, bend and break,
Iron bars will bend and break,
My fair lady.

Build it up with gold and silver,
Gold and silver, gold and silver,
Build it up with gold and silver,
My fair lady.

Every time "My fair lady" is sung, the arches of the bridge come down (the two children forming the bridge lower their arms), capturing a child inside. That child then takes the place of one of the children forming the bridge, and the child who is replaced goes to the end of the line.

Another Way to Play

- Walk under the bridge at first, but later children can march, jump, gallop, hop, or skip!

Capture the Kids

This game is a combination of London Bridge Is Falling Down (see page 63) and Statues (see page 76).

Why It's a Great Game

For cognitive development:
- Improving listening skills

For social/emotional development:
- Working with a partner
- Practicing leading and following
- Experiencing feelings of belonging

For physical development:
- Practicing starting and stopping
- Moving with a partner
- Performing low- to moderate-intensity physical activity

Content Areas
Language Arts
Music
Social Studies

How to Play

Materials
Cassette or CD player
Piece of moderately paced music

The children stand in two lines, facing each other. The first two children form an arch with their arms. The remaining children hold hands and, as the music plays, move in pairs under the arch, where they let go of their hands and move, each in their own direction, to the back of the line. (The child on the left moves down the left side of the line, and vice versa.) When you stop the music, the children under the arch are "captured." They become the arch, and the children acting as the original arch move to the end of the line and hold hands. The game continues at least until each pair of children has had a turn to be the arch.

Another Way to Play

- As in the variation for London Bridge Is Falling Down (see page 63), you can challenge the children to move in different ways as they travel under the arch. Possibilities include tiptoeing, marching, galloping, jumping, hopping, and skipping. Keep in mind the following: First, the skill you ask the children to perform should match the rhythm of the music; otherwise it will be too difficult. Also, moving in conjunction with a partner is more difficult than moving alone. Therefore, you should only invite the children to perform those skills you know they can both do well.

The Farmer in the Dell

This twist on the traditional game offers an opportunity for creativity and more movement! Before you begin, you may want to talk with the children about the actions of each of the various people/critters involved in the game.

Why It's a Great Game

For cognitive development:
- Learning about role playing/imagining
- Learning about the various roles in the game
- Experiencing patterning
- Experiencing rhyming

For social/emotional development:
- Creating feelings of belonging
- Increasing self-expression

For physical development:
- Performing low- to moderate-intensity physical activity
- Practicing a variety of movements

Theme
Occupations

Content Areas
Language Arts
Math
Music
Social Studies

How to Play

One child stands in the center of a large circle, mimicking the actions of a farmer. (These actions should be the child's choice and could include raking, milking a cow, riding a horse, riding a tractor, planting seeds, and so forth.) As the children circle the farmer, they sing the following song.

> **The Farmer in the Dell**
> *The farmer in the dell,*
> *The farmer in the dell,*
> *Hi-ho, the derry-o.*
> *The farmer in the dell.*
>
> *The farmer takes a partner,*
> *The farmer takes a partner,*
> *Hi-ho the derry-o.*
> *The farmer takes a partner.*

At the start of the second verse, the farmer points to another child to come into the center of the circle. That child must then perform the actions he imagines a farmer's partner would perform, as the farmer continues with his actions. The game continues with the following verses:

The partner takes a child...
The child takes a dog...
The dog takes a cat...
The cat takes a rat...
The rat takes the cheese.

At this point, all of the remaining children come into the circle and take on the shape of a piece or chunk of cheese! Then, ask the children to link hands and sing as they circle:

And now our farm's complete,
And now our farm's complete,
Hi-ho, the derry-o,
And now our farm's complete!

Another Way to Play

● If you have enough children, add some other farm animals, such as a cow, pig, duck, or chicken.

The Wheels on the Bus

This popular song is known primarily as a musical fingerplay. But, with a bit of a twist, it can become a participatory game involving a lot more movement.

Why It's a Great Game

For cognitive development:
- Learning about transportation

For social/emotional development:
- Experiencing a sense of belonging

For physical development:
- Practicing a variety of movements
- Performing low- to moderate-intensity physical activity

Theme
Transportation

Content Areas
Music
Social Studies

How to Play

Play this game the same as Follow the Leader (see page 40), with the children behind you in a single-file line. Then, with everyone singing the following verses, act out the appropriate accompanying movements.

> **The Wheels on the Bus**
> *The wheels on the bus go 'round and 'round,*
> *'Round and 'round, 'round and 'round,*
> *The wheels on the bus go 'round and 'round,*
> *All around the town.*
>
> Additional Verses
> *The wipers on the bus go swish, swish, swish…*
> *The doors on the bus go open and shut…*
> *The baby on the bus goes, "Wah, wah, wah…"*
> *The horn on the bus goes beep, beep, beep…*
> *The driver on the bus says, "Move on back…"*
> *The money on the bus goes clink, clink, clink…*

Another Way to Play

- Add an extra element to the game by "dropping the passengers off" one at a time. Choose various points throughout the room where you stop and march in place. Depending on the number of players and the number of stops you intend to make, you can call out the name of one or more passengers to depart. For example, you can call out, "Justin and Tina's bus stop!" When they hear their names, Justin and Tina leave the line, go to the assigned spot, and march in place. Continue until all of the passengers are off the bus. Then, while everybody waves, sing: *It's time for the bus to go on home…*

Row, Row, Row Your Boat

Like a fingerplay, this game involves putting actions to words. However, instead of just using hands and fingers, this game gets the whole body involved. The children can perform this game in a circle or by moving back and forth across the room, depending on the available space. Before beginning, talk to the children about rowing a boat and about the words *gently* and *merrily*.

Why It's a Great Game

For cognitive development:
- Learning about different forms of transportation
- Expanding vocabulary

For social/emotional development:
- Experiencing feelings of belonging

For physical development:
- Performing moderate-intensity physical activity
- Moving upper and lower torsos in different ways

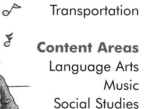

Theme
Transportation

Content Areas
Language Arts
Music
Social Studies

How to Play

As the children sing the following lyrics, they walk and perform a rowing action with their arms.

> **Row, Row, Row Your Boat**
> *Row, row, row your boat*
> *Gently down the stream*
> *Merrily, merrily, merrily*
> *Life is but a dream.*

Another Way to Play

- Change the lyrics so the children paddle a canoe or kayak, which is a different kind of motion. You might also pretend to sail, in which case the children can become either the boat or the sails.
- If you have scooters, the children can sit on them and pretend they're boats. Otherwise, use carpet squares.

Pop Goes the Weasel

You can either play a recording of this familiar song or sing the words.

Why It's a Great Game

For cognitive development:
- Improving listening skills
- Following directions

For social/emotional development:
- Experiencing feelings of belonging

For physical development:
- Jumping
- Developing muscular strength and endurance
- Starting and stopping
- Changing direction

Content Areas
Language Arts
Music

How to Play

Materials
Recording of "Pop Goes the Weasel" (optional)

Ask the children to walk as this song is played or sung, jumping lightly into the air every time they hear, "Pop!" If you have a large space, the children can walk freely. Otherwise, they should walk in a circle.

Pop! Goes the Weasel

All around the cobbler's bench
The monkey chased the weasel.
The monkey thought 'twas all in fun—
Pop! Goes the weasel.

A penny for a spool of thread
A penny for a needle.
That's the way the money goes—
Pop! Goes the weasel.

Another Way to Play

- Ask the children to jump and clap with each pop.
- Encourage them to jump and change direction with each pop.
- Challenge the children to freeze each time they hear the pop, and not move again until the next verse begins.
- If you're singing this song, change the tempo at which you sing.
- Add a parachute to the fun! Holding the chute in one hand, the children begin walking in one direction, at the same time singing or listening to "Pop! Goes the Weasel." They jump into the air, stop, change directions, or jump and change directions with each pop.

Rhythm Mimic

This game is similar to Movement Mimic (see page 21) but it specifically involves listening and rhythmic skills.

Why It's a Great Game

For cognitive development:
- Practicing sequencing
- Experiencing rhythm
- Improving auditory discrimination

For social/emotional development:
- Experiencing feelings of belonging
- Learning to cooperate
- Taking turns

For physical development:
- Practicing keeping the beat

Content Areas
Language Arts
Math
Music

How to Play

Sitting in a circle with the children, begin by choosing a simple rhythmic pattern (for example, two hand claps or three pats on the floor or lap) that each child must imitate in turn, until it comes back to you.

Another Way to Play

- As an alternative to clapping hands, use rhythm sticks to tap out the beats.
- As the children become more adept at this game, you can make it more challenging by beating out more complex rhythms. For example: 1l2, 1l2l3.
- Play a game of Echo, in which you clap out the syllables of everyone's name or of the lines of a nursery rhyme or poem—one clap per syllable—and the group echoes the rhythm.

Conga!

To adults, this is an activity that takes place at weddings—and, depending on your view of it, is either to be avoided or eagerly joined! But to the children it's just a fun game, like Follow the Leader (see page 40), that everyone will want to participate in!

Why It's a Great Game

For cognitive development:
- Following directions
- Replicating physically what the eyes see

For social/emotional development:
- Learning to cooperate
- Experiencing feelings of belonging

For physical development:
- Performing moderate-intensity physical activity
- Moving in various ways to the rhythm of the music

Content Areas
Art
Music
Social Studies

How to Play

Materials
CD or cassette player
Piece of lively music
    that lends itself
    to movement

Start the music and line up the children behind you, single-file, each with his or her hands on the hips of the child in front of him or her. Start to move around the room to the music, with the goal being for everyone to stay connected in the line. If children do fall out of line, however, they dance on their own!

Musical Hugs

This feel-good game is as simple as they come. Before you begin, you may want to discuss gentle and respectful hugging with the children.

Why It's a Great Game

For cognitive development:
- Developing listening skills
- Differentiating between sound and silence
- Practicing counting

For social/emotional development:
- Experiencing feelings of belonging
- Enjoying positive physical contact
- Learning self-expression

For physical development:
- Starting and stopping
- Performing moderate-intensity physical activity

Content Areas
Math
Music
Social Studies

How to Play

Materials
Cassette or CD player
Musical recording(s)

While the music is playing, the children move around the room any way they wish. When you stop the music, the children hug whoever is closest to them.

Another Way to Play

- For a slightly more challenging version of the game, ask two children to hug with the first round, three children to hug with the second round, four with the third round, and so forth, until there's just one big group hug!

Musical Chairs

In the traditional game of Musical Chairs, at the end of every round one more child is eliminated and required to sit against the wall and watch the other children continue to play. Children decide, "I'm a loser." "I'm not fast enough." "I'm not smart enough." It's a horrible feeling and one that every child would like to avoid. In order to do so, children may resort to using antisocial behaviors, as they poke, push, shove, or trip so they can continue "playing." By modifying the game to make it a cooperative activity, children learn prosocial behaviors and promote their problem-solving abilities, while having a wonderful time! Keep in mind, though: Even very young children have already been ingrained in the ways of competition and may not believe there are no losers with this game. If they are reluctant to move from the front of "their" chairs, encourage them to get going. Or, if there's another teacher or an aide available to control the music and chairs, join in the game!

Why It's a Great Game

For cognitive development:
- Developing listening skills
- Learning to discriminate between sound and silence
- Learning about problem solving

For social/emotional development:
- Learning to cooperate
- Experiencing feelings of belonging

For physical development:
- Practicing stopping and starting

Content Areas
Language Arts
Music
Social Studies

How to Play

Materials

1 chair for every child   Cassette or CD player   Recording of lively music

Arrange the chairs in a circle, facing outward, with one child standing in front of each chair. When the music starts, the children circle the chairs. When it stops, they sit in the chair closest to them. When the music starts again, you remove one of the chairs. Then, when it stops, the children must find a way to share the remaining chairs. This continues until there is only one chair left to share!
Note: Many possible solutions to this challenge exist (this is known as divergent problem solving). As an example, if each of the children places one big toe on the remaining chair, they've successfully met your challenge!

Another Way to Play

- Depending on the ages and skill levels of your children, you may want to start with an easier version of this game. Instead of chairs, use hoops laid flat on the floor. Then, challenge the children to share the remaining hoops/hoop.

Musical Magical Hoops

Musical Magical Hoops combines elements of Musical Chairs and Statues but, unlike those two games, this one also tests the children's memory. Before you play, determine what motor skill will be represented by what color hoop. For example, if you have hoops in red, blue, and yellow laid out, the red could indicate running in place, the blue might indicate shaking all over, and the yellow stretching. These will be the only skills allowed inside the hoops!

Why It's a Great Game

For cognitive development:
- Recognizing colors
- Improving listening skills
- Discriminating between sound and silence
- Improving memory skills

For social/emotional development:
- Practicing sharing space
- Experiencing the mood-altering properties of music

For physical development:
- Practicing stopping and starting on signal
- Performing moderate- to vigorous-intensity physical activity
- Practicing the designated motor skills

Content Areas
Art
Language Arts
Music

How to Play

Materials
Several plastic hoops, in three colors, scattered around the floor

While the music is playing, the children move in any way they want throughout the room. When the music stops (you press the pause button), they step into the closest hoop. For as long as the music is stopped, while inside the hoop, they perform the designated motor skill.

Another Way to Play

- When the children's memory skills are ready for a greater challenge, add hoops in more colors!

Musical Partners

Be sure to start and stop the music randomly, with various lengths of time for both the playing and the pauses. Long pauses will heighten the anticipation, and very brief ones will have the children squealing in delight.

Why It's a Great Game

For cognitive development:
- Improving listening skills
- Differentiating between sound and silence

For social/emotional development:
- Experiencing feelings of belonging

For physical development:
- Practicing stopping and starting
- Performing moderate- to vigorous-intensity physical activity

Content Areas
Language Arts
Music
Social Studies

How to Play

Materials
Cassette or CD player
Musical recording(s)

The children take partners. When the music starts, they move away from each other. When the music stops, they must quickly find each other, hold hands, and sit down until the music starts again.

Another Way to Play

- This game also can be played in two circles, one inside the other (one partner in the inside circle and one in the outside). When the music starts, the circles move in opposite directions. When it stops, the children run to their partners, hold hands, and sit down.

Statues

Asking children to move "in the way the music makes you feel" can be intimidating to some. But making a game out of "movement improvisation" relieves any possible fear of failure!

Why It's a Great Game

For cognitive development:
- Improving listening skills
- Discriminating between sound and silence
- Experiencing a variety of musical elements

For social/emotional development:
- Encouraging self-expression
- Practicing sharing space
- Experiencing the mood-altering properties of music

For physical development:
- Stopping and starting on signal
- Balancing
- Practicing a variety of movements and movement elements

Content Areas
Language Arts
Music

How to Play

Materials
Cassette or CD player
Recordings of songs that inspire a variety of movements
Ribbon streamers, chiffon scarves, or plastic hoops (optional)

Encourage the children to move while the music is playing and freeze into a statue when the music stops. Tell them to remain like statues until the music starts again! Randomly stop and start the music by pressing and releasing the pause button on your tape or CD player. Surprise the children by varying the amount of time you play and pause the music.

Another Way to Play

- Use a different style of music (a march, a waltz, an orchestral piece) every time you play the game—or during each game. You'll be amazed at how it changes the children's movements!

Body Part Boogie

This game is similar to Statues (see previous page) but more challenging because it requires children to isolate and use individual body parts. Even if children can't isolate the movement, they'll have fun trying.

Why It's a Great Game

For cognitive development:
- Identifying body parts
- Following directions
- Improving listening skills

For social/emotional development:
- Encouraging self-expression
- Experiencing the mood-altering properties of music

For physical development:
- Moving various body parts
- Practicing stopping and starting

Theme
My Body

Content Areas
Language Arts
Music
Science

How to Play

Materials
Cassette or CD player
Music in varying styles

Ask the children to stand in a circle or have them scatter throughout the room. Tell them they must stand completely still. Play a piece of music and designate just one body part for the children to move (for example, an arm, a head, a foot, a leg, fingers) to it. When you stop the music, they must freeze again. Use different styles of music to inspire different kinds of movement.

Another Way to Play

- For a challenge, assign different pieces of music to different body parts. In other words, when the children hear the classical piece, for example, ask them to move one arm. When they hear the rock-and-roll piece, they should move a leg, and so on.

Musical Movement

Starting with just two sounds helps ensure success with this game.

Why It's a Great Game

For cognitive development:
- Learning auditory discrimination
- Improving memory

For social/emotional development:
- Encouraging self-expression

For physical development:
- Practicing a variety of movements and movement elements

Content Areas
Language Arts
Music

How to Play

Materials
Variety of instruments

Assign different movements to different musical sounds. When the children hear each sound, they move in the appropriate way. For example, when you play the slide whistle, the children move up and down while standing in place; a heavy drumbeat tells them to stomp; striking a triangle means they tiptoe; and shaking a tambourine is the signal to shake their bodies!

Another Way to Play

Let the children choose their own ways to move to each sound.

Roll Over

Acting out the song "There Were Ten in the Bed" makes simple computation less abstract and more fun.

Why It's a Great Game

For cognitive development:
- Learning about subtraction

For social/emotional development:
- Learning to cooperate

For physical development:
- Practicing log rolls

Content Areas
Language Arts
Math
Music

How to Play

Have the children lie on the floor side by side, pretending they're in a big bed. As you and the children sing the following song, encourage them to roll over, with one child rolling further than the others on the fifth line of each verse sung. Begin the song with a number equal to the number of children playing.

There Were Ten in the Bed
There were ten [or the number of children playing] in the bed,
And the little one said,
"Roll over, roll over."
So they all rolled over,
And one fell out.

There were nine in the bed,
And the little one said...

There was one in the bed,
And the little one said,
"Alone at last!"

High & Low

In music, pitch is related to the highness or lowness of the notes. This game gives physical expression to what the children are hearing.

Why It's a Great Game

For cognitive development:
- Improving listening skills
- Recognizing pitch

For social/emotional development:
- Experiencing feelings of togetherness

For physical development:
- Experiencing moving through the levels in space (low, middle, and high)
- Performing moderate-intensity physical activity
- Improving flexibility

Content Areas
Art
Language Arts
Math
Music

How to Play

Materials
Slide whistle (optional)

Invite the children to crouch low to the floor. Using either a slide whistle or your voice (you can intone or hum), start low and gradually get higher and higher, asking the children to do the same. As the notes descend, the children do, too. As the notes rise, so do the children.

Another Way to Play

- An easier activity is to ask the children to sit and raise and lower their arms to the accompaniment of the ascending and descending notes.
- Pause every so often, causing the children to freeze. This helps them discriminate between sound and silence.

Limbo!

If you're using a rope and there isn't a second adult to hold the other end, secure one end to a bookshelf, doorknob, or something similar so all the children get to participate. Also, by using a long rope or pole, several children can participate at once. Two twists to this game make it different from the traditional—the children can go under in any way they wish (even crawling!), and, by slanting the rope or pole, you make it possible for all the children to succeed at any level.

Why It's a Great Game
For cognitive development:
- Reinforcing the concept *under*
- Encouraging problem solving

For social/emotional development:
- Experiencing success
- Experiencing feelings of belonging

For physical development:
- Improving flexibility

Content Areas
Language Arts
Music

How to Play

Materials
A long rope or pole

Put on a lively piece of music (preferably Latin). Hold the rope or pole high enough to allow the children to walk under it. After everyone's had a turn, lower it slightly. When it's becoming challenging for some children, angle the rope or pole, explaining that the children can go under it at any point.

Another Way to Play

- Invite the children to try going over the slanted rope or pole in any way they want, such as hopping, jumping, or leaping.

Cooperative Games

The prevailing belief is that competition is good for everyone—that being competitive is human nature. But is it human nature, or is it learned behavior? Kohn (1992) cites studies showing that, given a choice, most preschoolers prefer cooperative activities to competitive ones. And in a *New York Times* essay, Nicholas Kristof (1998) told a hilarious story about trying to teach the traditional game of Musical Chairs to a group of five-year-old Japanese children, who kept politely stepping out of the way so others could sit in their chairs.

Competition leads to antisocial behaviors (Kohn, 1992). Cooperation, on the other hand, fosters prosocial behaviors. Cooperation:

- is more conducive to psychological health.
- leads to friendlier feelings among participants.
- promotes a feeling of being in control of one's life.
- increases self-esteem.
- results in greater sensitivity and trust toward others.
- enhances feelings of belonging.
- increases motivation.

This chapter includes 16 cooperative games that help show children how good it feels to work and be together.

Monkey See, Monkey Do

The children play this game in pairs, standing about 12 inches apart and facing each other.

Why It's a Great Game

For cognitive development:
- Replicating physically what the eyes see
- Learning about the concept of mirror reflection

For social/emotional development:
- Learning to cooperate
- Accepting others' ideas
- Taking turns

For physical development:
- Practicing a variety of nonlocomotor movements
- Experiencing the concept of personal space

Theme
Family & Friends

Content Areas
Art
Science
Social Studies

How to Play

Materials
If desired, demonstrate the concept of *reflection* using a mirror (optional).

Ask one child to perform simple movements in place and encourage the second child to imitate the partner as a mirror reflection. At your signal, the children switch roles.

Another Way to Play
- Stand where all the children can see you easily. Move parts of your body in various ways slowly and without verbal instruction. Encourage the children to imitate your movements.

Bicycle Built for Two

Sing "Bicycle Built for Two," as the children play this game.

Why It's a Great Game

For cognitive development:
- Reinforcing the concept *around*
- Experiencing the concept *rotation*
- Learning about cycling as a form of transportation
- Counting

For social/emotional development:
- Learning to cooperate
- Experiencing feelings of togetherness
- Experiencing teamwork

For physical development:
- Building muscular strength and endurance

Themes
Family & Friends
Transportation

Content Areas
Math
Science
Social Studies

How to Play

Group the children in pairs. Partners lie on their backs with the soles of their feet together and "pedal." Invite them to count how many times they can go around without breaking contact.

Bicycle Built for Two
Daisy, Daisy, give me your answer, do.
I'm half crazy all for the love of you.
It won't be a stylish marriage.
I can't afford a carriage.
But you'll look sweet upon the seat
Of a bicycle built for two.

Switcheroo

When we ask children to take partners, they naturally choose their best friends first. But all too often, without intending to be cruel, children hurt one another's feelings by refusing to be someone's partner. Because this activity is so much fun, children will be more concerned with how quickly they can find a partner than who their partner is.

Why It's a Great Game

For cognitive development:
- Identifying body parts
- Improving listening skills
- Identifying left and right (for those developmentally ready)

For social/emotional development:
- Learning to cooperate
- Accepting others

For physical development:
- Practicing turning
- Using various body parts
- Performing bursts of moderate-intensity physical activity

Themes
Family & Friends
My Body

Content Areas
Language Arts
Science
Social Studies

How to Play

Designate an area in the room (preferably in the middle) to be the "Lost and Found," and explain to the children that if they can't find a partner quickly enough, they should go to Lost and Found. There, other children who haven't yet found partners will be waiting to join up with them! Begin the game with partners standing back to back. When you call out the name of a body part (or parts), the children turn to face each other, briefly connect those parts, and return to their back-to-back position. When you call out "Switcheroo!" children must get back-to-back with a new partner, and the game begins again as you call out more body parts. Possible "connections" include the following:

- Hands (both, right, or left)
- Elbows
- Wrists
- Big toes
- Right or left shoulders
- Right or left ankles
- Knees
- Feet
- Thumbs
- Pointer (or other) fingers
- Right or left hips
- Noses (gently!)

Another Way to Play

- Make the game more challenging by playing it in trios, or asking children to connect non-matching body parts (for example, a hand to a knee; an elbow to a hip).

It Takes Two

This partner activity poses two challenges to the children: They must remain connected, and they must discover how many ways they can move while connected.

Why It's a Great Game

For cognitive development:
- Identifying body parts
- Solving problems

For social/emotional development:
- Learning to cooperate
- Accepting others' ideas

For physical development:
- Experiencing a variety of movements, levels, and directions
- Increasing flexibility

Themes
Family & Friends
My Body

Content Areas
Science
Social Studies

How to Play

Challenge the pairs to connect various body parts—one set at a time—and to find how many different ways they can move without breaking the connection. When they've had ample time to explore the possibilities, invite them to try another set of body parts. Possible connections include:
- right (left) hands
- both hands
- right (left) elbows
- both elbows
- one or both knees
- right (left) feet
- backs

Another Way to Play

- As an alternative, suggest non-matching body parts, like a hand to an elbow, a hand to the back, or a wrist to a shoulder.

Footsie Rolls

This game requires a lot of cooperation, as well as enough room to move safely. If you have a small area for movement, limit the number of participants to one pair at a time, with the remaining children acting as the audience, cheering or applauding while the partners remain connected and groaning when the connection is broken.

Why It's a Great Game

For cognitive development:
- Solving problems
- Experience with *impetus* and *momentum* (see Glossary on page 131)

For social/emotional development:
- Learning to cooperate
- Learning about teamwork

For physical development:
- Practicing log rolls
- Improving coordination

Theme
Family & Friends

Content Areas
Science
Social Studies

How to Play

Materials
Carpeted surface or mat

Partners lie on their backs, with the soles of their feet touching. The object of the game is for the children to see how far they can roll without their feet breaking contact. It's difficult, but fun!

Another Way to Play

- Once partners have mastered rolling in one direction, challenge them to try it in the other direction.

The Snake

Talk to the children about snakes and other creatures that move along the ground, explaining that this type of movement is known as *slithering*.

Why It's a Great Game

For cognitive development:
- Learning about snakes and other slithering creatures
- Exploring the word *slither*
- Solving problems

For social/emotional development:
- Learning to cooperate
- Learning about teamwork

For physical development:
- Experiencing movement at a low level
- Practicing crawling

Themes
Family & Friends
Animals (Reptiles)

Content Areas
Language Arts
Science
Social Studies

How to Play

Help the children pair off, stretching out on their stomachs, one in front of the other. The child in back takes hold of the ankles of the child in front, forming a two-person "snake." The object of the game is for the snake to see how far it can slither without breaking apart.

Another Way to Play

- Once the children have mastered the challenge of slithering in pairs, invite the two-person snakes to connect with other two-person snakes and to practice slithering at twice their original lengths. Eventually, challenge the children to keep connecting until they've formed one big snake!

Keep It Afloat

Ask the children for their thoughts on why most things that go up into the air—including themselves, but excluding such things as birds and airplanes—don't stay in the air!

Why It's a Great Game

For cognitive development:
- Learning about the concepts *flotation* and *gravity*
- Solving problems
- Improving spatial awareness

For social/emotional development:
- Learning to cooperate
- Taking turns

For physical development:
- Improving eye-hand coordination
- Improving visual tracking
- Performing upper torso exercise

Theme
Family & Friends

Content Areas
Science
Social Studies

How to Play

Materials
1 inflated balloon for every 2 children

Give each pair of children an inflated balloon and challenge them to keep it in the air for as long as they can, without either of them touching it twice in a row. (In other words, they have to take turns tapping it.)

Another Way to Play

- Give the children an allotted amount of time in which to volley the balloon (say, one minute), using a beginning and ending signal. Ask them to count the number of times they tap the balloon to keep it afloat for that minute.
- Challenge the children to keep the balloon afloat with any body part but their hands! Or, you can specifically assign the parts they're to use—for example, elbows, heads, or knees.
- When the children are able to play this game without bumping into each other, you can have them play it in groups of three, none of whom can touch the balloon twice in a row.
- Give a group of three children two balloons to keep in the air.

Pass It On

This game starts simply enough but can be made increasingly challenging!

Why It's a Great Game

For cognitive development:
- Problem solving
- Sequencing

For social/emotional development:
- Learning to cooperate
- Learning about teamwork

For physical development:
- Improving coordination
- Improving balance
- Improving eye-hand (or eye-foot) coordination

Theme
Family & Friends

Content Areas
Math
Social Studies

How to Play

Materials
1 beanbag or small ball per group

The object of this game is for the children to pass the beanbag (or ball) from person to person without letting it drop. Start with the children standing in a circle. One child holds the beanbag and passes it to the child either to his right or left. The process continues until the beanbag has come full circle. Then, another child passes the beanbag in the opposite direction. When the children are ready for a new challenge, ask them to pass the beanbag using only the backs of their hands.

Another Way to Play

- Add an extra element of challenge by inviting the children to gently toss, rather than pass, the beanbag. Because the children will be standing side by side, they can toss the beanbag lightly a few inches into the air in the direction of the next child.
- Have the children form two lines facing each other and standing less than 12" apart. Invite them to toss the beanbag back and forth, zigzagging down the lines.
- Challenge the children to pass the beanbag from and to the top of the foot. (This one requires lots of balance!)
- Invite the children to pass the beanbag using other body parts. Possibilities include knees, elbows, and shoulders.

Sticky Popcorn

Talk to the children about the process of cooking popcorn—from kernels in the oil, through heating up, to becoming full–fledged pieces of popcorn. What would happen if something sticky, like butter or caramel, was poured all over the popcorn?

Why It's a Great Game

For cognitive development:
- Learning about the cooking process
- Reinforcement of the concepts *up* and *down*

For social/emotional development:
- Learning to cooperate
- Experiencing feelings of togetherness

For physical development:
- Practicing moving from a low level to a high level in space
- Jumping
- Building muscular strength and endurance
- Performing moderate- to vigorous-intensity physical activity

Themes
Family & Friends
Nutrition

Content Areas
Art
Math
Science
Social Studies

How to Play

Invite the children to get on the floor, in the smallest shapes possible, imagining they're tiny uncooked kernels of popcorn. Then the "oil" they are soaking in starts to heat up, and they start popping. They keep popping all over the room! "Pour" butter or caramel all over them, making them very sticky. When that happens, every time they come near another kernel, they stick to it until there's just one big, stuck bunch of popcorn!

Beanbag Freeze

This game requires the children to walk around the room with a beanbag balanced on a specific body part. If the beanbag falls, the player has to freeze in that spot and wait until another player has retrieved the beanbag for her or him. If the second player's beanbag also falls, that player freezes, too, until help comes along.

Why It's a Great Game

For cognitive development:
- Solving problems

For social/emotional development:
- Learning to cooperate
- Being helpful
- Being patient

For physical development:
- Balancing
- Improving coordination
- Practicing the ability to be still

Theme
Family & Friends

Content Areas
Science
Social Studies

How to Play

Materials
1 beanbag per child

Hand out the beanbags and explain the rules to the children. Invite them to balance the beanbag on a fairly simple body part, such as their palms or backs of the hands. Then give them the signal to go!

Another Way to Play

- Make this game even more challenging by asking the children to balance the beanbags on the tops of their heads, shoulders, or elbows.

Three-Legged Creatures

The object of this game is for two children to maneuver together as one three-legged creature. It should get their heart rates up and the giggles going!

Why It's a Great Game

For cognitive development:
- Solving problems
- Counting

For social/emotional development:
- Learning to cooperate
- Learning about teamwork
- Being patient
- Developing a sense of humor

For physical development:
- Improving balance
- Improving coordination
- Performing moderate- to vigorous-intensity exercise

Theme
Family & Friends

Content Areas
Math
Social Studies

How to Play

Materials
1 long scarf for every 2 children

With the children paired up and standing side by side, gently tie their inside legs together with the scarf. Challenge the children to count how many steps they can take in a predetermined amount of time; then give them the signal to go!

Another Way to Play

- This game lends itself to practicing other locomotor skills besides walking. Challenge the children to perform on three legs the other skills they're able to perform alone. Possibilities include jumping (in this case, on three feet), hopping (on two feet, lifting either the inside or outside legs), galloping (with either the inside or outside feet leading), and skipping. (**Note:** Don't invite them to try this unless they can skip on both sides of the body with the correct rhythm, which most children can't do until they're at least five years old.)

Body Balance

The object of this game is for the children to work together to maintain a steady balance—not to throw one another off balance!

Why It's a Great Game

For cognitive development:
- Counting
- Experiencing the concept of time

For social/emotional development:
- Learning to cooperate
- Learning about teamwork

For physical development:
- Improving balance
- Improving body control

Theme
Family & Friends

Content Areas
Science
Social Studies

How to Play

Standing in a circle, the children each place their hands on the shoulders of the children on either side of them. They then rise onto tiptoe and count the number of seconds they can remain still.

Another Way to Play

- Instead of touching shoulders, ask the children to hold hands or put their arms around each other's waists.
- Ask the children to rise onto tiptoe and count aloud as they lower their heels. For example, as you count out four seconds, they lift their heels. Count another four seconds, during which they hold still. And during the final four seconds, they lower their heels. The higher the number and the more slowly you count, the more challenging this exercise becomes.
- Make the balancing more challenging by asking the children to stand on one foot, to extend one leg into the center or to the outside of the circle, or to lean forward or backward. All of these movements can be performed either flat-footed or on tiptoe.

Ducks, Cows, Cats, and Dogs

Talk to the children about each of the animals named in the title of this game adapted from Docheff (1992). (If you're playing with very young children or a small group, choose only two or three of the animals named in the title.) Ask the children what sounds they make.

Why It's a Great Game

For cognitive development:
- Improving auditory discrimination
- Learning about various animals and their sounds
- Counting

For social/emotional development:
- Learning to cooperate
- Developing a sense of humor

For physical development:
- Practicing cross-lateral movement
- Moving at a low level in space

Theme
Family & Friends

Content Areas
Language Arts
Math
Science

How to Play

With the seated children scattered throughout the room, whisper the name of one of the animals in each player's ear. Once each child has been assigned an animal, ask the children to get on their hands and knees and close their eyes. When you give the signal to start, they begin moving about the room with their eyes still closed making the sound of their animal and trying to find the other animals like them. (Let the children know when all the cats, for example, have found each other. They can sit and watch the others who are still searching.) When all the animal groups have found one another, ask the children to count the number of "animals" in their group.

Another Way to Play

- If you're playing this game with older children—or with children who have played the original version often—add other animals to the mix. Just make sure they're animals with familiar sounds, such as chickens, pigs, or sheep.

Palm to Palm

This game requires the children to respect each other. Children should have some experience with cooperative activities before trying this game.

Why It's a Great Game

For cognitive development:
- Reinforcing the concept *around*
- Counting

For social/emotional development:
- Learning to cooperate
- Learning empathy for the visually impaired

For physical development:
- Improving spatial awareness
- Turning

Theme
Family & Friends

Content Areas
Math
Social Studies

How to Play

Help the children pair off and stand facing one another with arms extended and palms touching. They then drop their arms to their sides, close their eyes, turn around, and try to once again touch palms with their eyes closed!

Another Way to Play

- Once the children can do this, challenge them to turn around more than once before reconnecting with their partners! See how many times they can turn around and still come back together.

Up We Go!

This is easier said than done!

Why It's a Great Game

For cognitive development:
- Reinforcing the concepts *up* and *down*

For social/emotional development:
- Learning to cooperate

For physical development:
- Practicing moving through the levels (low, middle, and high) in space
- Building muscular strength and endurance

Theme
Family & Friends

Content Areas
Language Arts
Math
Social Studies

How to Play

Partners sit back to back, with their elbows linked, and try to stand up. If they succeed, encourage them to try to sit back down while their elbows are still linked.

Let's Make a Machine

This game explores the concept that it takes many parts to make up a whole. If you have an especially large group of children, get two or three "machines" going to limit children's waiting time.

Why It's a Great Game

For cognitive development:
- Learning about machinery

For social/emotional development:
- Learning to cooperate
- Learning about teamwork
- Taking turns

For physical development:
- Practicing nonlocomotor movement
- Performing repetitive exercise

Theme
Family & Friends

Content Areas
Science
Social Studies

How to Play

One child begins by repeating a movement that can be done while remaining in one spot, such as raising and lowering one arm. A second child joins in, standing near the first and contributing a different movement that relates in some way, without interfering, with the first. (For example, if the first child were raising and lowering an arm, the second child might move her arm in, underneath the first child's raised arm, and out.) One after another, the children join in, each contributing a functioning part to the "machine." (The machine can take on any shape, growing in different directions.) Once the machine is fully formed, each "part" should make a sound that represents its movement.

Another Way to Play

- For children with more experience with cooperative activities, add another element to this game by requiring that there be at least one contact between parts. In other words, each child must touch at least one other child while moving.

Outdoor Games

There are so many reasons why children should spend as much time outdoors as possible. It is the best place for young children to practice and master emerging physical skills and to experience the pure joy of movement. It's the place where they're likely to expend the most energy—and where they can engage in loud and messy behaviors considered inappropriate for indoors!

The outside light stimulates the pineal gland, which is the part of the brain that helps regulate our biological clock, is vital to the immune

system, and simply makes us feel happier. Outside light triggers the synthesis of vitamin D. And Jensen (2000) cites a number of studies that found lack of outdoor light lowered student learning and productivity.

Then, too, there's the aesthetic value of the outdoors. Because the natural world is filled with amazing sights, sounds, and textures, it's the perfect resource for the development of aesthetics in young children. Because aesthetic awareness means a heightened sensitivity to the beauty around us, it is something that can serve children well at those times when, as adolescents and adults, the world seems less than beautiful.

Finally, Rivkin (1995) tells us there's one very basic reason why children need to experience being outside: humans evolved in the outdoors. Thus, we have a link with nature that can't be replaced, and in fact, will be atrophied by technology. She wonders if, lacking intimate association with nature, we can still be human.

The following chapter offers 24 games that, due to the space required, lend themselves to outdoor play. But don't limit yourself to playing only these games outdoors. Whenever possible, you and the children should "take it outside!"

Bubble Chase

There's nothing like a bubble chase to inspire children to run and jump! But with this game, the emphasis is on cooperation so that children avoid the typical collisions.

Why It's a Great Game

For cognitive development:
- Experiencing the concepts *flotation* and *evaporation*
- Counting and adding

For social/emotional development:
- Cooperating
- Learning about teamwork

For physical development:
- Performing moderate- to vigorous-intensity physical activity
- Running and jumping
- Building muscular strength and endurance

Content Areas
Math
Science

How to Play

Materials
A bottle of bubbles

Stand where all the children can see you and blow one "batch" of bubbles at a time. Each time a child pops a bubble, he counts it, increasing the previous number by one. For example, if Antonio pops the first bubble, he calls out "one." If Lena pops the second bubble, she calls out "two." The twist is that no child is allowed to pop two bubbles in a row. But they can still take part in the chase!

Cat and Mouse II

This simple game of tag involves lots of action, constant participation by everyone involved, and squeals of delight.

Why It's a Great Game

For cognitive development:
- Experiencing the concepts *chasing* and *fleeing*
- Learning about cats and mice

For social/emotional development:
- Experiencing feelings of belonging
- Developing a sense of humor

For physical development:
- Running and dodging
- Performing moderate- to vigorous-intensity physical activity

Theme
Animals

Content Area
Science

How to Play

In this variation of Cat and Mouse I (see page 16), one child is designated as the Cat, while the rest of the children act as Mice. The object of the game is for the Cat to catch a Mouse. The Mouse who gets tagged becomes the Cat, and the original cat becomes a Mouse. The new Cat can tag anyone except the child who was just Cat, which allows all children to be more involved in the game.

Freeze Tag

Although this game requires players to be sedentary for moments at a time, they are never eliminated. And, if their fellow players do their job, they will get back in the game quickly.

Why It's a Great Game

For cognitive development:
- Experiencing motionlessness versus motion

For social/emotional development:
- Cooperating
- Being helpful

For physical development:
- Performing moderate- to vigorous-intensity physical activity
- Running and dodging
- Stopping and starting

Content Areas
Science
Social Studies

How to Play

One player is "IT." Tagged players must remain frozen, feet apart, until another player crawls under their legs! If IT can freeze everybody, the last person to be frozen gets to be IT for the next game.

Another Way to Play

- Turn this into a game of "Food Tag" or "Book Tag" by requiring the child "unfreezing" another child to touch the "frozen" child and call out the name of a food or book simultaneously, such as "scrambled eggs" or "The Tiny Seed." The hardest part is that the name of a food or book can only be used once.
- On a sunny day, play a game of Shadow Tag, in which IT has to tag a player by stepping on her shadow. When a child is tagged, she's frozen until another player steps on her shadow.

Turtle Tag

Children will love this new twist on an old game.

Why It's a Great Game

For cognitive development:
- Solving problems
- Learning about turtles

For social/emotional development:
- Cooperating

For physical development:
- Practicing running and falling
- Performing moderate- to vigorous-intensity exercise

Theme
Animals

Content Areas
Science

How to Play

This game is played just like the traditional game of Tag, with two exceptions: First, if a child is being chased, she can be "safe" by lying on her back like an upside-down turtle; and second, the game is timed. If "IT" hasn't tagged someone in a certain amount of time, say, a minute and a half, at the sound of your signal, IT should get in the "turtle position." Then, choose another child to be IT.

Another Way to Play

- Add a cooperative element to this game by requiring the "turtles" to remain on the ground until another player comes along to help them up!

Elbow Tag

This game of tag is more difficult because children must run while they are "attached" to someone else!

Why It's a Great Game

For cognitive development:
- Solving problems

For social/emotional development:
- Cooperating

For physical development:
- Running
- Practicing moving with a partner
- Performing moderate- to vigorous-intensity exercise

Content Area
Social Studies

How to Play

Players are paired off. All but two of the children link arms. Of the two without arms linked, one is "IT" and the other is the person IT is going to chase. At your signal, everyone starts to run! The child whom IT is chasing tries to hook onto one of the linked pairs. If he manages to link his elbow with someone else's, he and the child he's linked with become a new pair; and the child on the opposite side of them is set free to become the child being chased. If IT tags the child being chased before she can link with someone, she and IT reverse roles. But, because they're in such close proximity at this point, an immediate tag-back wouldn't be fair. So the game should pause temporarily, allowing IT and the "chasee" to separate. You then give the signal for everyone to start running again.

Reverse Tag

Instead of the child who is "IT" doing the chasing and everyone else fleeing, IT is the one running away! This variation on an old game means continuous participation for all.

Why It's a Great Game

For cognitive development:
- Counting
- Solving problems

For social/emotional development:
- Experiencing feelings of belonging

For physical development:
- Running and dodging
- Performing moderate- to vigorous-intensity physical activity

Content Areas
Math
Social Studies

How to Play

Everyone but "IT" counts to five, during which time IT runs as far away from the group as possible. Then, all the other children chase IT. The child who manages to tag IT then becomes IT and must run away from everyone else.

Blob Tag

A simple modification to an old game keeps all of the children participating and active.

Why It's a Great Game

For cognitive development:
- Learning about addition

For social/emotional development:
- Experiencing feelings of belonging
- Cooperating

For physical development:
- Performing moderate- to vigorous-intensity physical activity
- Running and dodging

Content Areas
Math
Social Studies

How to Play

Choose one child to be "IT." Everybody tagged also becomes IT. The result is a cluster of children that keeps growing until there's just one big "blob" running around together. The last person tagged is the first person to be IT in the next round.

Another Way to Play

- For a more challenging version, have tagged players hold hands with IT and all others tagged.

Seaweed Tag

This is another version of tag that keeps everyone moving! Explain to the children what seaweed is and show them pictures, if possible.

Why It's a Great Game

For cognitive development:
- Following directions
- Learning about certain elements of the ocean

For social/emotional development:
- Experiencing feelings of belonging
- Learning about teamwork

For physical development:
- Running and dodging

Theme
The Ocean

Content Areas
Science
Social Studies

How to Play

Materials
Pictures of seaweed (optional)

Mark off a large area to serve as the "ocean." The area should be large enough so the children can run and dodge safely, but not so large that tagging becomes impossible. One child, acting as "seaweed," stands in the middle of this area, with the rest of the children (the "fish") lined up on one end of the ocean. At your signal, the fish try to cross the ocean. If tagged by the seaweed, they also become seaweed but they must keep one foot planted on the ground at all times. Those fish who make it to the other side now try to cross again. The game continues until all the fish have become seaweed! The last fish tagged is the first to act as seaweed for the next round.

Tail of the Snake

Expect screams and squeals as the children try to meet the challenge of this cooperative tag game.

Why It's a Great Game

For cognitive development:
- Reinforcing the concepts *front* and *back*

For social/emotional development:
- Cooperating
- Learning about teamwork
- Experiencing feelings of belonging

For physical development:
- Performing moderate- to vigorous-intensity physical activity
- Running and dodging

Theme
Animals (Reptiles)

Content Areas
Math
Science
Social Studies

How to Play

The children line up single file, each with hands either on the shoulders or the hips of the child in front (whichever is easiest). At your signal, the player in front (the head of the snake) tries to tag the player at the end of the line (the snake's tail)—without the snake coming apart! If the snake does come apart, the children should quickly try to put it back together again. If the player in front manages to catch the snake's tail, he goes to the end of the line and becomes the tail for the next round.

Duck, Duck, Goose II

This variation of Duck, Duck, Goose (see page 15) is played in pairs, which means there's lots of activity for everybody.

Why It's a Great Game

For cognitive development:
- Improving listening skills

For social/emotional development:
- Cooperating
- Enjoying humor

For physical development:
- Chasing and fleeing
- Performing moderate- to vigorous-intensity physical activity

Content Areas
Language Arts
Social Studies

How to Play

Materials
Masking tape, chalk, or 2 jump ropes

Using masking tape, chalk, or jump ropes, mark two lines about 10–15 feet apart. These lines designate the "safety zones." Divide the children into pairs, with each pair standing facing each other, in the center of the two safety zones. At your signal, the children take turns tapping each other on the shoulder, saying either "duck" or "goose." Nothing happens with the word "duck." But when one of the children says "goose," she has to turn around and run toward her safety zone, with her partner chasing her. If her partner tags her before she gets to the safety zone, when they return to the center, the partner gets to start the next round. If her partner is unable to tag her before she reaches the safety zone, she gets to start the next round when they return to the center.

Messy Backyard

This game is typically played with regular playground balls or wads of paper, but both of those can hurt if they accidentally hit a child. The chiffon scarves are much more difficult to throw for distance (they tend to float rather than fly), but they'll require a lot more muscle power.

Why It's a Great Game

For cognitive development:
- Reinforcing the concept over
- Counting

For social/emotional development:
- Learning about teamwork

For physical development:
- Throwing
- Performing upper torso exercise

Content Areas
Language Arts
Math

How to Play

Materials
1 chiffon scarf per child
Masking tape, chalk, or jump rope
Timer

Make a line with the tape, chalk, or rope (the line should be about equal to the length of half of the group lined up side by side).Then divide the children into two groups—one on each side of the line. Place an equal number of chiffon scarves on either side of the line. Set the timer. At your signal, the children race to pick up the balls or scarves on their side of the line and throw them onto the other side of the line. When time is up (say, two minutes), count the number of scarves on each side. Then divide them equally and start all over again!

Wall Ball

Young children are able to throw for distance before they can throw for accuracy. But if all they have to do is hit the side of a building, the chances are good that they will be accurate with their throws.

Why It's a Great Game

For cognitive development:

- Experiencing *cause* and *effect*
- Experiencing the concept *ricochet*

For social/emotional development:

- Experiencing success

For physical development:

- Throwing

Content Area
Science

How to Play

Materials
1 large, lightweight ball per child
A windowless outside wall

Line up the children, side by side, opposite a wall (the side of a building). Give each child a ball and explain that all they have to do is hit the wall with the ball. After each throw, players retrieve their own balls and try again, moving further away from the wall as they gain confidence.

Bowling

Typically, bowling requires tremendous eye-hand coordination and a lot of waiting. But young children aren't particularly adept at either (eye-hand coordination isn't fully developed until 9 or 10 years old, and we know how they feel about waiting). This game involves larger objects than the standard bowling ball and pins and is played in pairs.

Why It's a Great Game

For cognitive development:
- Experiencing *cause and effect*

For social/emotional development:
- Learning to cooperate
- Learning about teamwork

For physical development:
- Practicing ball rolling
- Improving eye-hand coordination
- Improving visual tracking

Content Areas
Science
Social Studies

How to Play

Materials
2-3 large, empty soda bottles per pair of children
1 beach ball or large playground ball per pair

Arrange two or three soda bottles in close proximity for each pair of children, and give each pair a ball. One child stands near the "pins" while the other bowls, that is, rolls the ball and tries to knock the bottles down. The second child then retrieves the ball while the first resets the pins. Then the second child takes a turn at bowling. The children continue in this manner, taking turns for as long as they stay interested.

Hoops II

"Hoops" is a nickname for the game of basketball. But because everything about the real game is too advanced for young children, this game will give them a chance to at least say they played a game that involves throwing something through a hoop.

Why It's a Great Game

For cognitive development:
- Reinforcing the concept *through*

For social/emotional development:
- Cooperating
- Taking turns

For physical development:
- Practicing underhand throwing
- Improving eye-hand coordination

Content Areas
Language Arts
Math
Social Studies

How to Play

Materials
1 plastic hoop per pair of children
1 small ball or beanbag per pair of children

Divide the children into pairs, and give each pair a hoop and a ball or beanbag. One child stands a few feet away from her partner, holding the hoop upright. The other child has the ball (or beanbag), which he tosses through the hoop. Partners take turns holding the hoop and tossing the beanbag. As the children become comfortable, they can move further away from the hoop.

Another Way to Play

- Play this game by (gently) kicking the ball through the hoop.

Ring Toss

At a carnival, the ring toss involves a very small ring being tossed onto a very small peg, which reduces the opportunity for success—even for adults! This game significantly increases the chance that the children will succeed.

Why It's a Great Game

For cognitive development:
- Reinforcing the concepts *over* and *around*

For social/emotional development:
- Experiencing success

For physical development:
- Attempting to throw underhand
- Improving eye-hand coordination

Content Areas
Language Arts
Math

How to Play

Materials
1 large, empty soda bottle or plastic cone per child
1 plastic hoop per child

Line up the soda bottles or plastic cones side by side and spaced far enough apart so plastic hoops placed over them don't interfere with each other. Line the children up similarly, each opposite a bottle or cone (and only a short distance away!), and give each child a hoop. Encourage the children to try to toss their hoop over the cone or bottle opposite them. After every unsuccessful try, they simply retrieve the hoop and try again. With each successful try, they can take a step further away from the cone or bottle if they desire.

Hopscotch

The traditional objectives of this game are to toss a marker (a flat stone, a beanbag, and so on) onto each numbered square consecutively, to hop onto the single squares without putting the second foot down, and to skip the square where the marker has landed. Children who fail to meet these objectives are eliminated from the game. But none of these objectives is as important as children having the opportunity to practice the many motor skills involved. So just let the children play—without any penalties paid! Also, children waiting should be invited to encourage their friends by cheering and applauding their efforts. Remember, however, that waiting is hard for young children—and it doesn't do anything to promote fitness—so if you have a large group, create more than one hopscotch grid.

Why It's a Great Game

For cognitive development:
- Recognizing numbers
- Counting
- Sequencing

For social/emotional development:
- Learning to take turns
- Encouraging others

For physical development:
- Jumping, hopping, turning, and basic underhand throwing
- Improving balance
- Improving muscular strength and endurance

Content Area
Math

How to Play

Materials
Chalk
Flat, paved area
Beanbag or other marker

With chalk, draw one or more hopscotch grids on the playground surface or a sidewalk (10 squares, numbered consecutively, with the numbers 1, 2, 5, and 8 in single squares and the numbers 3 and 4, 6 and 7, and 9 and 10 in side-by-side squares).

The children line up single file, and the first child tosses either a small stone or a beanbag (whatever you've designated) onto the square marked with the number 1. He then hops over that square (when possible, there should be no touching down on the square with the object on it), lands on one foot in the square marked 2, jumps in the squares marked 3 and 4 (a two-footed landing with the left foot in the left square and the right foot in the right square), hops (one-footed landing) in the square marked 5, and so on, up the grid. At the top of the grid, he turns and follows the same pattern back to the beginning, once again hopping over the first square. The second child then tosses the object into the square marked 2, and the process continues.

Another Way to Play

- Play this game indoors by using numbered carpet squares. But whether you play it indoors or out, as the children begin to excel at this game, make it more challenging by encouraging them to perform it at a faster tempo!
- Use letters instead of numbers in the squares to help children with the alphabet. Ask them to say the letter aloud as they move onto each square.

Jump the Rope

This simple game gives children an excuse to do one of their favorite things—jump!

Why It's a Great Game

For cognitive development:

- Sequencing

For social/emotional development:

- Practicing taking turns

For physical development:

- Improving eye-foot coordination
- Improving rhythm
- Practicing jumping
- Building muscular strength and endurance
- Performing moderate-intensity physical activity

Content Area
Math

How to Play

Materials

A jump rope, approximately 5–8 feet long

Have the children form a large circle, with children at arms' length from their neighbors. Stand in the center, holding one end of the jump rope with the other end lying on the ground (a plastic one with handles works well for this game). Start turning yourself around so the rope passes one child's feet at a time. The children jump over the rope as it reaches them.

Another Way to Play

- When the children become accomplished at this, pick up the pace!

Picture This

Sometimes we go through life without even noticing the things around us. But that's not the way it's supposed to be! This game gives children a reason to take notice.

Why It's a Great Game

For cognitive development:
- Identifying objects

For social/emotional development:
- Appreciating the outdoors
- Taking turns

For physical development:
- Performing moderate- to vigorous-intensity physical activity

Theme
Nature/Our
Environment

Content Areas
Science
Social Studies

How to Play

Materials

Pictures or photos of things found in your outside play area (for example, a tree, slide, swing, fence, bush, and so on)

Box

Place the pictures in the box, and place the box in the center of the play area. Line up the children in two single-file lines, on opposite sides of the box and several feet from it. Designate which line is to start first. The first child in the first line runs to the box, takes out a picture, looks at it, drops it back in the box, and then runs to the object pictured.

After touching the object, she runs to the end of her line. Meanwhile, as soon as she drops the picture back in the box, the first child in the second line runs to the box and repeats the process. Continue this at least until every child has had a few turns.

Ready, Set, Jump

It is in the outdoors that children are best able to practice large-muscle movement and to expend the most energy. This game gives them a reason to do both!

Why It's a Great Game

For cognitive development:
- Following directions

For social/emotional development:
- Experiencing feelings of belonging

For physical development:
- Practicing a variety of locomotor skills
- Improving spatial awareness
- Performing moderate- to vigorous-intensity physical activity
- Building muscular strength and endurance

Content Area
Science

How to Play

Select a starting point and two spots on the playground, somewhat equidistant from the starting point, that can serve as markers (for example, the swing set, the oak tree, or the monkey bars). At your signal, the children walk rapidly toward the first marker and jump from there to the second, and then jog back to the starting point. They can repeat these actions for as long as they stay interested, or you can substitute any other locomotor skills with each round of play.

Another Way to Play

- You can make this a relay race of sorts by lining the children up and having them complete the "course" one at a time, tagging the next child in line upon return to the starting point. So that the waiting children aren't sedentary, have them perform in place the locomotor skill the active player is doing. In the above example, they'd walk, jump, and jog in place, in that order.

Marco Polo

Often played in pools and lakes, this game is also suited to large outdoor spaces.

Why It's a Great Game

For cognitive development:
- Improving auditory discrimination

For social/emotional development:
- Feeling empathy for the visually impaired

For physical development:
- Improving spatial awareness

Content Areas
Language Arts
Social Studies

How to Play

Ask all the children except one to stand and close their eyes. The remaining child, who is "IT," chooses a spot to stand, at a distance from the other players. The players then repeatedly call out "Marco," to which IT responds "Polo." Using their listening skills only, the players must try to find IT. The first child to do so becomes the next IT.

Another Way to Play

- This can also be played as a partner game, with one partner trying to find the other. To make it a bit easier to play among a group of children, assign each pair different code words. For example, one pair could be "Marco Polo," another "Christopher Columbus," another "Lewis and Clark," and so forth. Or they can simply use their own first names!
- When the children have had ample experience with this, ask everyone to say "Marco Polo." This will require superior listening and voice recognition skills.

Red Rover

In the traditional version of this game, children stand in two side-by-side "teams" facing each other. Players on both sides hold hands. One player from one team calls for a player from the other team to be sent over. That child must then run, as forcefully as possible, toward the other side, trying to break through the barrier created by two children holding hands. If he succeeds, he and one of the players from the opposing team go back to his team. If he fails, he joins the team he was unable to break through. There are a number of problems with this from a whole-child perspective. Children who are thought to be the weakest are called upon first. Similarly, they look to break through what they believe to be the weakest link in the opposing team. And, of course, children get hurt. This modified version feels good and offers an educational component and an opportunity to practice motor skills.

Why It's a Great Game

For cognitive development:
- Improving listening skills
- Improving color discrimination
- Counting

For social/emotional development:
- Experiencing feelings of belonging

For physical development:
- Practicing a variety of locomotor skills
- Improving spatial awareness

Content Areas
Art
Language Arts

How to Play

The arrangement remains the same, with the children standing in two side-by-side lines facing each other. (Holding hands is optional.) Children take turns being the "caller" (perhaps moving from left to right down each line). But before the caller says anything, you designate the way in which the children are to move to the other line. (Possibilities include: tiptoeing, jumping, hopping, skipping, galloping, backward, sideways, crouching, and so on.) The child whose turn it is calls out, "Red Rover, Red Rover, send [blue] right over," choosing any color she wants. All the children on the other side wearing blue—anywhere on their outfits—cross over to the other line, in whatever way you've designated, and join the players on that side. The game continues with a player in the second line calling out a different color. (No color can be used twice in a row.) When the children determine that "all" the colors have been called, the game is over!

Another Way to Play

- Change the game to involve concepts other than color. For example, use letters if the children know the letters in their names. Use numbers to indicate the number of siblings or pets a child has (include "0").
- To make the game more challenging, ask the children to walk lightly, jump heavily, run slowly, tiptoe quickly, or gallop in zigzags.

Mother, May I?

In the original game, the person acting as "Mother" gives directions to one player and then, depending upon her whim, decides whether or not to allow that player to follow them. If she decides to allow it, the player must ask, "Mother, may I?" If he forgets, he has to go back to the starting line. The first player to reach Mother wins. Not only can this involve favoritism on Mother's part, it also involves a whole lot of waiting for the rest of the children.

Why It's a Great Game

For cognitive development:
- Improving listening skills
- Following directions
- Counting

For social/emotional development:
- Experiencing feelings of belonging

For physical development:
- Practicing variety of movements and directions

Content Areas
Language Arts
Math

How to Play

Acting as Mother, stand facing the children, about 20 feet away. Give an instruction for the children to take a certain number of a certain kind of movements. For example: "Children, take 5 steps on tiptoe." Or: "Children, take 3 jumps backward." The children then ask, "Mother, may I?" before doing as directed. The game continues until the children reach you. You can then start again with someone else acting as Mother!

What's the Time, Mr. Dog?

The traditional game is called "What's the Time, Mr. Wolf?" But because wolves have been given a bad reputation throughout history (they don't really eat children!), the players in this new version have been changed from a wolf and children to a dog and cats. Also, the traditional verse eliminated those children who were caught by the "wolf."

Why It's a Great Game

For cognitive development:
- Following directions
- Learning about cats and dogs

For social/emotional development:
- Experiencing feelings of belonging
- Enjoying humor

For physical development:
- Practicing tiptoeing and running
- Practicing stopping and starting

Theme
Animals

Content Area
Science

How to Play

Acting as the "dog," stand with your back to the children, about 20 feet away. The children, pretending to be cats, begin sneaking up on you, periodically asking, "What's the time, Mr. Dog?" You then turn around and give a time (any time will do: 3:00, 12:15, and so on). As soon as you turn around, the children must remain completely still. If you turn around and say, "Dinner time," you start chasing the "cats," who must run back to the starting line, where they're safe from the dog! You can then start the game all over again, with someone else playing the dog.

Another Way to Play

- Encourage the children to play the game on all fours.

Crossing Over

This game is a combination of Mother, May I? (see page 125), and Red Rover (see page 124).

Why It's a Great Game

For cognitive development:
- Identifying colors
- Improving listening skills

For social/emotional development:
- Experiencing feelings of belonging

For physical development:
- Running and dodging

Content Areas
Art
Language Arts

How to Play

Designate a starting and ending line, with the children standing side by side on the starting line. Stand in the center of the playing area, facing the children. They call out, "Is it safe to cross over?" You respond by saying, "Only if you're wearing [green]." The children wearing the color you've indicated can walk safely to the other side. But the children who aren't wearing that color have to try to get to the other side without you tagging them. If you do tag them, they stay in the center with you and also become taggers.

References

Bredekamp, S., & C. Copple, (Eds.). 1997. *Developmentally appropriate practice in early childhood programs.* Washington, DC: National Association for the Education of Young Children.

Butler, S. 2005. Circle time is the right time. *Early Childhood News,* 17(1): 28-30.

Coulter, D. J. 1995. Music and the making of the mind. *Early Childhood Connections: The Journal of Music- and Movement-Based Learning,* 1, 22-26.

Docheff, D. M. 1992. *Hey, let's play! A collection of P.E. games and activities for the classroom teacher.* Elma, WA: Dodge R Productions.

Jensen, E. 2000. *Learning with the Body in Mind.* San Diego, CA: The Brain Store.

Kohn, A. 1992. *No contest: The case against competition.* Boston: Houghton Mifflin.

Kristof, N. "Correspondence--Uncompetitive in Tokyo; In Japan, Nice Guys (and Girls) Finish Together." *New York Times,* April 12, 1998, p. 7.

Orlick, T. 1982. *The second cooperative sports & games book: Over two hundred noncompetitive games for kids and adults both.* New York: Pantheon.

Pica, R. 2004. *Experiences in movement: Birth to age eight.* Clifton Park, NY: Delmar Learning.

Rivkin, M.S. 1995. *The great outdoors: Restoring children's right to play outside.* Washington, DC: National Association of the Education of Young Children.

Rui Olds, A. 1994. "From cartwheels to caterpillars: Children's need to move indoors and out." *Child Care Information Exchange,* 97, May/June, p. 32-36.

Staley, L., & P.A. Portman. 2000. Red Rover, Red Rover, It's Time to Move Over! *Young Children,* 55(1): 67-72.

Williams, N.F. 1994. The Physical Education Hall of Shame, Part II. *Journal of Physical Education, Recreation & Dance,* 65(2): 17-20.

Resources for Playing With Children With Special Needs

The following books offer activities and information concerning games for children with special needs. Although all were published at least 10 years ago, they are considered classics in the field, as they have withstood the test of time.

Creative Play Activities for Children With Disabilities: A Resource Book for Teachers and Parents by Lisa Rappaport Morris & Linda Schulz. Champaign, IL: Human Kinetics, 1989.

Games for People With Sensory Impairments: Strategies for Including Individuals of all Ages by Lauren J. Lieberman & Jim Cowart. Champaign IL: Human Kinetics, 1996.

Inclusive Games: Movement Fun for Everyone! by Susan L. Kasser. Champaign IL: Human Kinetics, 1995.

The following books on play include comprehensive chapters on play and children with special needs:

Play and Child Development by Joe L. Frost, Sue Wortham, & Stuart Reifel. Upper Saddle River NJ: Merrill Prentice Hall, 2001.

Supporting Play: Birth through Age Eight by Dorothy Justus Sluss. Clifton Park NY: Delmar Learning, 2005.

Glossary

Cross-lateral movement. Moving the right arm and left leg, or vice versa, at the same time. Crawling is an example of cross-lateral movement.

Elements of movement. Describe how a movement is performed. If we liken movement education to the study of grammar, the skills themselves (e.g., running and jumping) can be considered verbs, while the six movement elements (space, shape, time, force, flow, and rhythm) are the adverbs modifying them.

Flow. One of the six elements of movement, flow is either bound (interrupted or punctuated movement) or free (uninterrupted movement). Impetus. A driving force.

Laterality. Understanding that the body is divided into right and left halves.

Levels in space. A subcategory of the element of space, levels are the planes—low, middle, and high—at or through which an individual can move. When standing upright, one is at the middle level. Anything closer to the ground is considered the low level. Positions or movements performed on tiptoe or in the air occur at the high level.

Locomotor skills. Movements that transport the body as a whole from one point to another. Sometimes referred to as traveling skills, examples are walking and hopping.

Momentum. The force of motion acquired by a moving body, as a result of impetus applied.

Nonlocomotor skills. Movements performed in place. They involve the axis of the body rotating around a fixed point. Examples are bending, stretching, and twisting.

Pathways. A subcategory of the element of space, pathways of traveling movements are either straight, curving, or zigzagging.

Shape. The element of movement describing the various shapes it is possible for the body to assume.

Index

P

Palm to Palm, 98
Parachute Lady (Guy) Says, 32
Parachutes, 26–36
Pass It On, 91
Pathways, 131
Patience, 35, 94–95
Patterning, 65–66
Personal space, 84
Physical development, 14, 37, 49, 53–54, 69, 85, 92–93, 99, 100, 103, 118–120, 122
Physical Education Hall of Shame, 9, 15
Picture This, 121
Pictures
    outdoor play area, 121
    seaweed, 110
Plastic
    animals, 51
    cones, 117
    hoops, 25, 52, 55, 73–74, 76, 116–117
Play and Child Development by Joe L. Frost et al., 130
Poles, 81
Pop! Goes the Weasel, 69
Portman, P.A., 9
Positional concepts, 42, 48, 52, 63, 80–81, 85, 111, 113, 117
Positive physical contact, 59, 72
Prepositions, 16, 18
Problem solving, 24, 27, 48, 55, 73, 81, 87–91, 94–95, 106–108
Punchinello, 24

R

Ready, Set, Jump, 122
Recorded music, 20, 64, 69, 71–77, 81
Red Light, Green Light, 47
Red Rover, 9, 11, 124, 127
Relay Race, 9
Repetitive exercise, 100
Reptiles, 89, 111
Resources, 130
Respecting others, 55
Reverse Tag, 108
Reviewing learning experiences, 24
Rhyming, 24, 62, 65–66
Rhythm, 43, 70–71, 95, 120
Rhythm Mimic, 70
Rhythm sticks, 43
Ribbon streamers, 76
Ring Around the Rosie, 62

Ring Toss, 117
Rivkin, M. S., 102
Role playing, 65–66
Roll Around, 35
Roll Over, 79
Ropes, 81
Rotate It, 26–27
Row, Row, Row Your Boat, 11, 68
Rui Olds, A., 37
Running, 103–112, 122, 124, 126–127

S

Scarves, 76, 95, 113
Science, 17, 26–31, 33–34, 39, 42, 51, 68, 77, 84–90, 92–95, 96–97, 100, 103–106, 110–111, 114–115, 121–122, 126
Seasons, 29
Seaweed Tag, 110
Self-awareness, 24, 38
Self-concept, 39
Self-confidence, 48
Self-control, 47
Self-esteem, 83
Self-expression, 58, 65–66, 72, 76–78
Sensitivity, 83
Sequencing, 14, 17, 19–21, 50, 53, 70, 91, 118–120
Sequential memory skills, 23
Sequential movement, 14
Shadows, 42, 105
Shapes, 45, 56
    defined, 131
Sharing space, 40, 43, 45–46, 55, 74, 76
Shrinking Room, 55
Simon Says, 9, 31–32, 39
Sitting in the Dark, 60
Sleeping Giants, 49
Slide whistles, 78, 80
The Snake, 89
Snakes, 89, 111
Snow, 29
Social studies, 14, 18–19, 21–22, 25–27, 29, 32–36, 38, 41–42, 44, 46–48, 51–53, 55, 57–60, 64–68, 71–73, 75, 84–100, 105, 107–112, 115–116, 121, 123
Social/emotional development, 14
Soda bottles, 115, 117
Songs
    "Bicycle Built for Two," 85
    "The Farmer in the Dell," 65
    "Head, Shoulders, Knees, and Toes," 38